Vindicated

Vindicated

CONFESSIONS OF A VIDEO VIXEN, TEN YEARS LATER

KARRINE STEFFANS

BENBELLA

BenBella Books, Inc.
Dallas, TX

BenBella Books, Inc.
10300 N. Central Expressway
Suite #530
Dallas, TX 75231
www.benbellabooks.com
Send feedback to feedback@benbellabooks.com

Printed in the United States of America
10 9 8 7 6 5 4 3 2 1

Library of Congress Cataloging-in-Publication Data:
Steffans, Karrine, 1978-
Vindicated : confessions of a video vixen, ten years later / Karrine Steffans ;
foreword by Datwon Thomas.
pages cm
ISBN 978-1-940363-82-0 (hardback)—ISBN 978-1-940363-92-9 (electronic)
1. Steffans, Karrine, 1978- 2. Actors—United States—Biography. 3. Stripteasers—
United States—Biography. I. Title.

PN2287.S6765A3 2015

791.4302'8092—dc23

[B]

2015006607

Editing by Leah Wilson
Copyediting by Eric Wechter
Proofreading by Michael Fedison and Cape Cod Compositors, Inc.
Text design by Silver Feather Design
Text composition by PerfecType, Nashville, TN
Cover design by Kit Sweeney
Jacket design by Sarah Dombrowsky
Cover photography by Jamal Bayette
Printed by Lake Book Manufacturing

Distributed by Perseus Distribution
www.perseusdistribution.com
To place orders through Perseus Distribution:
Tel: (800) 343-4499
Fax: (800) 351-5073
E-mail: orderentry@perseusbooks.com

Significant discounts for bulk sales are available. Please contact
Glenn Yeffeth at glenn@benbellabooks.com or 214-750-3628.

Several names in this book have been changed,
not to protect them but to protect myself.

Finally.

To every man and woman who has battled domestic violence and lost and to the ones who, by the grace of God, came up against it and won, this little piece of triumph is for you.

Aeron: The Celtic god of slaughter.

CONTENTS

Foreword: And How   xiii
DATWON THOMAS

Introduction: The Truth about Things   1

Chapter One: Eight   5

Chapter Two: With a Kiss   11

Chapter Three: Thieves in the Temple   19

Chapter Four: Breathe   27

Chapter Five: Overjoyed   33

Chapter Six: Rings and Things   39

Chapter Seven: And He Held Me   47

Chapter Eight: Lovers and Brothers   55

Chapter Nine: Fear and Loathing   61

Chapter Ten: Things We Lost   67

Chapter Eleven: Soap Operas and Porn   73

Chapter Twelve: What Has Changed   85

Chapter Thirteen: Son of a Bitch   95

Chapter Fourteen: With a Vengeance   103

Chapter Fifteen: The Unraveling   109

Chapter Sixteen: Order of Protection   121

Chapter Seventeen: Same Tune   131

Chapter Eighteen: It Was All So Ridiculous   137

Chapter Nineteen: And Again   145

Chapter Twenty: The Way Out   155

Chapter Twenty-One: Passion Fruit   161

Chapter Twenty-Two: Proof of Life   167

Chapter Twenty-Three: Loser   173

Chapter Twenty-Four: Mercy   179

Chapter Twenty-Five: Do the Work   187

Chapter Twenty-Six: Apropos   193

Conclusion: The Beginning   199

About the Author   203

FOREWORD

And How

I have a confession of my own . . .

I have never read *Confessions of a Video Vixen*. Nope. Not once. While the average reader and music industry insider soaked up all the high drama of the *New York Times* best seller filled with family shame and secrets, kidnapping, rape and rap, infidelity, drugs, liquor and projectile champagne, love, war and backstabbing, lashing lyrics, fetishes, and the occasional good time associated with the *Scarlet Letter*–like tome . . .

I knew the real.

I knew the person *behind* the Karrine Steffans persona.

How am I so sure I knew the person beneath the surface with a character like her? Someone who has been able to hide her feelings and expose truths at the same time? Trust me, it's been a long and revealing road to learning who that person is outside of the headlines and heartache.

A mutual friend, a television and radio host, introduced us over ten years ago. He warned, "She's a lot to deal with. Proceed with caution." I didn't know how right he was. I was editor-in-chief of *KING* magazine, the top publication for scantily clad urban-edged celebrity models at the time. After our mutual friend introduced us over the phone, I was in direct contact with the infamous Steffans.

During our initial conversation she was brash, funny, and straightforward. "Look," she said, "just hit me when you get out here to LA. We're gonna do it up!" She was the famed music industry enchantress; her name was starting to bubble in the urban entertainment industry because of her prowess and the powerful men she dated. Both men and women were fascinated with her—obsessed even. Everyone wanted to have her. Many were leery of her and tread lightly when mentioning her name. I just wanted to know the story; how could a whole industry be on pins and needles from one petite video model?

The story was, she packed way more of a powerful punch than her frame would let on. Her strength came from being fearless in the face of danger, or maybe she was just plain crazy. But the thing is, sometimes people who seem crazy aren't all that crazy—just different. Once Karrine and I actually got together and hung out, without all the fanfare, gossip, and labels, I got to know an intently driven individual. A hard-core bookworm with a vast knowledge of the written word and a personal library that rivals some educational scholars'. Someone with a flair for the perfect placement of everything from furnishings to publicity and an eye for interior design. An intense conversationalist with a degree in strategy and seduction.

I've also gotten to know each side of her multifaceted personality.

I've seen her wild out in a public parking lot during a magazine photo shoot, laughing uncontrollably, snatching the wig off her head, running in a circle, and yelling obscenities at everyone within earshot. I've seen her get into a verbal altercation in the wee hours of the morning at a West Los Angeles IHOP restaurant filled with celebrities that escalated from harmless banter to an all-out food fight where she was throwing scalding tea at the head of her target, dodging lemons heaved by her opponent—an incident that gave me the best laugh of my life.

I've seen her masterfully plot out her vision for the release of *Confessions*, before it was even completed. Everything from the talking points for the book tour to, "I'm gonna be on *Oprah*! Watch!" I thought she was insane to even mention sharing the same rare air as the media queen, only to watch Karrine on television, months later, sitting across from Ms. Winfrey, telling her life's tale of despair and debauchery and ultimate survival.

But why did she give all of this sacred information from the bowels of entertainment's secret society and good-ol'-boys club? Why be so candid and raw about herself, her flaws and misjudgments, her growing pains and blind ambition?

At one time I thought it was for fame.

I now know it was a cry for help.

She sought validation of her existence not only in her writing, but in the arms of various superstars of stage and screen. For her, those relationships were therapy for a soul lost in its own body, a soul traumatized by an adolescence so cruel that she was never given the chance to see things clearly while becoming a young woman. When you are accustomed to abuse, mistreatment becomes part of your being—you need it to function—and until you are able to realize your own dysfunction, you are destined to repeat it.

At some point, it's time for self-healing.

But that didn't happen for Karrine, not completely and not right away. She dove deeper into the abyss of abnormal love/hate shit. When you've taken on a beast of an industry and survived, you tend to come out of it feeling invincible. And she did. Yet, the battle she waged was fought with side arms that weren't really real to begin with. The armor in which she warred was weighted with emotional baggage from years past and she was gathering even more luggage along the way. So, when Karrine brought that mangled, burdened woman into new situations, like multiple snap-decision marriages, they could have never been good for her. She continued to gravitate to abuse as a normal condition, living in it silently for years.

The world continued to be fascinated with the persona, knowing very little about the person.

But I knew.

To further complicate matters, the commitment of a joint union like marriage, which is supposed to be pure and untainted, could never be such for Karrine, as it was always overshadowed by her one true love's constant presence.

Lil' Wayne.

I've seen Karrine speak of physical torture and tattered spirit, only to mention the Young Money rapper's name and instantly light up with positivity. I've also seen her cry a wail of despair only a soul mate can when Wayne was reportedly on his deathbed and gone to the world. I've seen them fall apart and come back together and I've seen him save her. He was the only one who could rip her from the clutches of an abusive first marriage, keep her from settling into obscurity yoked to an unequal second husband, and then jar her out of a writer's block that threatened her career and her livelihood—all without knowing he'd done such.

Which brings us to present day, ten years after shocking the world with a book so groundbreaking it needed the follow-up you are reading now. I've since moved on from those wild days of *KING* magazine, where Karrine and I concocted landmark photo shoots and interviews. Friends and associates have come and gone in this past decade, yet one individual continues to stay in constant contact, whether I'm running the ship at a newer, hotshot place of business or trudging through the dogged days of creating my own empire. That person is Karrine Steffans, and I'm proud to say, Karrine, with your evolution into who you are today, you've come a long way, baby.

Speak your truth, Karrine, as your story seems to set yourself and others free.

DATWON THOMAS
February 2015

P.S. Hey, folks . . . I'm gonna read this one. "And how!"

The Truth about Things

I have had this book swirling in my mind for years. I have been writing its words and naming its chapters for nearly a decade, honing what I would relay to you when the time finally came to write it all down. As I lived it, I gathered every hurt, every slander, every libelous fabrication and erroneous notion, and I just stored them away. As much as I wanted to fight in the war waged against me, I was too weak. I knew I wouldn't be able to write about this particular time in my life until I was over it.

So, I waited.

I waited seven years.

Then, I began to write.

My strokes were swift and intense as I pounded the words of this book onto the keyboard of my computer, racing to deliver to you the truth, finally. The writing went on for weeks and the weeks turned into a month and then two.

Then, suddenly, I stopped.

The penning of this memoir didn't come as easily as I thought it might. After all those years of holding in so much truth, I thought I'd be bursting at the seams with emotion and the need for resolve. I thought I'd be thrilled to release the anguish and anxiety I had swallowed and stomached for the better part of a decade, prancing around the world as if nothing could hurt me, but being broken all the while.

This was my moment!

This was my vindication!

With this book, if I could just finish it, everything would begin to make sense. With it, I could turn my mess into a message and if, or when, I managed to do so, it would be impossible to regret even one day of my life.

To be vindicated is to be shown to be right, reasonable, or justified, and after nearly a decade of living under the physical and emotional tyranny of one man, I know what it is like to be discredited by an abuser, as he points the finger at you so that no one will believe your story. There are millions of women like me and many of them die at the hands of such men and many others resort to taking the lives of their abusers. It is by the grace of God that I am here today and it is by His grace that I can tell my story, that I can show other women just how bad it can be and then, just how good it can get.

But first, I had to get past my sadness and finish this book. Page after page, the words poured out. One paragraph became many, pages turned into chapters, and those chapters became this book. It was all in perfect form and looked just as a book should, but toward the end, I found it difficult to move forward.

The last one hundred pages were the hardest.

But why?

I knew how the story ended. I lived it! I knew the people, the places, and the dates. I kept records. It wasn't some sort of mechanical writer's block; it was an emotional block, and because of it, this book almost didn't happen. It took a strenuous, nearly unbearable amount of soul searching in order for me to come to grips with what it is about this memoir, out of all my memoirs, that made it almost impossible to finish. It took me a couple weeks of introspection and the baring of truths before I came to an astonishing conclusion.

I'm not over it.

When horrible things happen, when we make bad decisions and suffer reprehensible repercussions, we can never just get over it. Still, as a survivor, I moved forward with my life, picking up the pieces along the way, pulling proverbial thorns from my side and broken teeth from my mouth. I patched my wounds and bandaged my heart, but I can never, ever get over what has been done. Abuse stays with us forever, it becomes part of our fabric, and the guilt I felt for putting myself in such a position stayed with me, still stays with me. As much as I thought I'd moved past what had been done, writing this book proved to me just how lasting the effects of domestic violence are and can be.

It will always be sad.

The recollections in this memoir are my saddest, and it took me quite a while to realize that as I was tap, tap, tapping on my computer's keyboard, I was also refusing to acknowledge that sadness. I refused to connect with my words and to feel the way I felt during the days and years I was writing about. This was becoming the first memoir I had ever written without shedding a tear and I just couldn't do that to you.

I couldn't do it to myself.

So, I wrote my way through the pain, and this book became such a source of catharsis. As I rounded the bend and finished the last few chapters, I couldn't help but hope that my words, my unabashed truth would also vindicate *you*. I couldn't help but hope that, if you are a victim, you will read my truths and they will become yours. I pray that even if no one else believes you, you will know that I believe you and that, somehow, you will derive the strength you need to save your life, all because of this little book.

Here's to hope.

CHAPTER ONE

Eight

"One thousand-seven, eight, nine, two thousand," I counted aloud, as I shuffled the crisp one-hundred-dollar bills. "Two thousand? What the fuck?" I searched the rumpled sheets on the bed for my mobile phone and upon finding it, anxiously dialed Bruce's number.

"Hello," he answered, already knowing why I was calling.

"There's only two thousand dollars here! I need eight hundred more dollars!" I explained, angered, feeling tricked. He knew what I needed and had already made me wait for weeks before loaning me the money, only to short me.

"Well, that's all I can do," he began. "You're not the only person who needs help; you're not the only one with problems. I'm helping a lot of other people, too, you know, and I can only do what I can do."

That was bullshit.

Bruce was happy to do what I needed him to do as long as I did as he said, but now I wasn't living by his specifications. He liked the control he had over me. Even though he was engaged to another woman, he was possessive and jealous of me, and since I'd let my ex-husband, Aeron, back into my life and home, Bruce was punishing me to prove just how powerful he was.

And he did it with $800.

Eight.

The number of new beginnings.

I hung up the phone and began pacing the carpeted floor of my bedroom, knowing I was running out of time, knowing everything was about to change—again. But, even though things would soon come crashing down around me, I didn't panic. Instead, I became numb. It was the accumulation of many years of bad luck based on a series of terrible decisions and unfortunate events. I'd brought it all upon myself years before, when I made one fateful and nearly deadly decision. By now, I'd made so many mistakes along the way that I had no choice but to depend on other people, on men, to help me survive, and now I was at their mercy.

Aeron had given me money earlier that month for groceries, utilities, and the car payment. He'd done what he could and I wouldn't have been able to make it through the past few months without him. Bruce wasn't enough, though he thought he was everything. But now, eight hundred dollars short, I wouldn't be able to pay the rent and it was already one week late. In most cases, this wouldn't be a big deal, but I'd already received a three-day notice and the company that ran the complex where I lived was known for some of the fastest evictions in the city.

By the end of the month, I'd have to start packing.

There were only three weeks until my next payday, and even though I knew it wasn't about the money for him, I couldn't believe Bruce would short me, even with the promise of repayment in just a few weeks. There was nothing I could do—nothing but make plans to pack up and leave.

Over the next few weeks, Aeron floated in and out of my place, sleeping next to me at night, knowing I needed help but unable to do any more for me. I had always been the breadwinner, always the one caring for him, spending my last dime supporting us, my son and his, saving him every time he needed saving. But now that I needed him to save me, he couldn't. He was always inept. Still, there he was, lying next to me as my ship slowly sank, just waiting to jump that ship the moment its nose touched the water.

This was the story of our relationship.

In the following weeks, as my time ran out, Aeron drove me around town, looking at homes and apartments for lease. We talked about getting a place together and splitting the rent, now that he was working. During our four years together, he rarely worked and when he did, his contribution to the household bills always fell short.

Splitting rent would be an anomaly.

He filled my head with hope as we searched for the right place for our children and us. I scoured the Internet for a space large enough and in the right neighborhood, a place with newer construction, and the perfect kitchen for preparing family dinners. I printed out leads and organized them by city. I called renters and agents and made appointments to view each and every home or unit that was right for us. I had the two thousand dollars Bruce gave me to put toward the move and was depending on Aeron to manage the rest.

I was depending on him but nothing came of it.

Soon, the day came to move out of my apartment and I had nowhere to go.

I rented a storage unit nearby and employed the same moving crew I'd hired many times before. They came into my apartment and began breaking down the beds and hauling out my furniture. My son, Naiim, pitched in by packing up his clothing, books, and games. Aeron, however, just stood there in the middle of the living room, talking on the phone. He'd been unable to qualify for a place for us to live and frankly, even if he had, he couldn't afford the move. He'd been living with his mother, sister, brother, and friends in the year since we divorced and was always a rambling man—even when we were together.

Now, he was on the phone pretending to try to find some money and a place for us to live, but it was all an act—everything was an act with him. He had no intention of helping me do anything more than the minimum, just as Bruce had no intention of helping me the way he promised as long as Aeron was helping me at all. Both of them weren't enough and I was so far from being enough for myself.

With all the packing and hauling going on, it frustrated me to see my big, strong ex-husband standing in the middle of the living room, refusing to lift a finger. "Why don't you get the fuck off the phone and help!" I shouted. "Everyone here is doing something and you're just fucking standing there being big and fucking black! If you're not going to help, get the fuck out and talk on the phone somewhere else!"

Aeron finally disconnected his call and engaged with me but not in the way he should have. He began yelling back at me, inching closer as I stood in the kitchen, emptying the cabinets. He towered over my tiny body with his six-foot-four-inch frame and screamed at me about screaming at him right before balling up his fist and punching right through the pantry door. Splinters flew and his hand bled as he extracted his fist from the particleboard. All I could do was look at him.

Numb.

This is how he'd always been. This is why we were no longer together and now, this was why we couldn't even be friends. I knew right then, in that instant, that our relationship, on all levels, was over.

"Really?" I asked. "Did you *really* just punch a fucking cabinet, you weirdo?"

"It's just that you were yelling at me," he explained.

"I wouldn't give a shit what I was doing! I can say *anything* I want! I can yell as much as I want! But what you *don't* get to do is go around punching shit! Now, get out of my way so I can finish packing."

Eager to show he was of some use, Aeron walked into my son's room and began helping him pack. When he was finished, he walked out onto the patio and got back on his phone. Walking into Naiim's room after Aeron stepped out, it was easy to spot which box he packed, with its lopsided tape barely sealing it shut. Ripping off the tape and opening it, I found an assortment of items strewn about— clothing, books, video games, and even my son's laptop, which he used every day to complete his homeschool lessons. I shook my head in disgust and emptied the box, repacking each item in other, appropriate boxes, leaving the laptop out for my son's daily use. I didn't say a word. I had already reached my decision. I got myself into this mess, I was about to get myself out of it, and I wasn't about to take Aeron with me.

I was done making the same mistakes.

Over the next two days, the movers and I worked diligently to empty my apartment and pack everything into two storage units. Aeron did what he did best—disappeared. He stopped by toward the end of the second day to see how everything had gone and help with whatever minimal work was left before leaving, again. During our last night in the apartment, with all my furniture in storage, Aeron went out and bought an inflatable bed and a few blankets on which my son and I could sleep. He had nothing else to offer us. No room and board, no reprieve, no solace, just an air mattress and a few thin blankets. After the homes, the cars, and all the comfort I'd offered him over the years, now, in my time of need, he had so very little to give. I lay there that night, overwhelmed with disgust, determined to do better but not knowing how.

The following morning, my teenage son and I cleared out what was left in the apartment and shoved it all into my car, then into the storage unit. We struggled to move heavy television sets and other bulky items, but we made it happen, until all that was left in the apartment was a four-hundred-dollar juicer I bought for Aeron sometime during our marriage. I placed it in the middle of the living room, walked out the front door, and locked it. I was leaving the apartment a day ahead of schedule and didn't alert Aeron to my departure. I delivered my keys to the leasing office and rode away from the complex, not knowing what was ahead.

Later that day, Aeron slipped his key into the lock to find me gone and the juicer there in my stead. Not knowing where I was, he called to inquire. "Where are you guys heading?" he asked.

"A hotel," I answered, vague and disconnected.

"Okay, well, call me when you get there and let me know where you guys are."

"Sure. I will. Take the juicer and return your keys to the office."

"Yeah. Doing that, now."

"Okay, good. I'll call you later."

I hung up the phone as I coasted down the highway, headed to a hotel way on the other side of town, knowing I wouldn't be calling him, ever.

It was September 2012, and I was homeless.

CHAPTER TWO

With a Kiss

*I*t was July 10, 2007, and my life seemed perfect. As I drove away from my hairdresser's shop, my mobile phone rang. I answered it to find my publicist, Danika Berry, on the other end of the line. "Hey, Danika," I said.

"Hey, K. Where are you?" she asked.

"Ummm . . . I'm at the corner of Olympic and La Brea. Why? What's up?"

"Perfect. I'm at this event at a spa, called Le Vie L'Orange, on Robertson Boulevard, and it's really dead. Can you stop by?"

"Yeah. Sure. It's on my way home, so I'll stop by for a second."

"Oh my God, thank you so much. See you in a minute."

It was a hot summer day. My hair was freshly curled and my brand-new white Range Rover was newly detailed and glimmering in the Los Angeles sunshine. My sunroof was open and my music was blaring, the bass of my custom woofers announcing my arrival everywhere I went. Life was good and I was happy. Ecstatic. I had everything I wanted in life. I was a fixture on the *New York Times* Best Sellers list with my first book, *Confessions of a Video Vixen*, and with its proceeds, I'd recently purchased my first home, worth over one million dollars, on the hillside of a Los Angeles suburb, complete with a pool and all the privacy I needed for skinny-dipping. I was poised to publish my second book, *The Vixen Diaries*, and was on the cover of *KING* magazine with the headline ". . . the Bitch is Back." I was floating. My life and the publishing industry had been good to me. I had just bought the custom Range Rover and also owned a brand-new Mercedes Benz SL550, each worth over one hundred thousand dollars. My son was enrolled in and attending the best school in the city and we needed for nothing. Professionally and financially, I had everything I'd ever dreamed of, plus a thriving relationship with entertainment's foremost rising star, Lil' Wayne.

Wayne and I had been dating since the beginning of 2007 and, though I was madly in love with him, there was a lot to be desired about being with a rapper who practically lived on his tour bus and traveled the world, sleeping with a different woman most every night. Still, he and the friendship we forged was important to me and I wasn't prepared to let him go—not then, not ever.

On top of the world, I sauntered into the event and was instantly met by Danika and entertainment columnist Jawn Murray. Soon after arriving, my friend Omarosa Manigault showed up and soon it was like a family reunion. I wasn't concerned with the spa or the event itself, but was content to just sit and chat with my friends. Still naive to the weight of my presence, I never realized that I was the main attraction that afternoon. I never realized what an oddity I was and how seeing me out and about was like happening upon a unicorn.

I never understood my worth.

About an hour after my arrival, I heard another familiar voice among the small group of people in attendance and knew instantly to whom the booming, attention-seeking voice belonged. Aeron Killian was a former child star, all grown up and living life as a series of stereotypes. He stood six-feet-four-inches tall, with dark brown skin, hands like a silverback gorilla, and a deep, bass-filled voice. Aeron and I had met seven years prior, in June 2000, at a local barbershop and hair salon, and instantly upon meeting him, I found him annoying. He had to cause a scene everywhere he went; he had to be the loudest and the center of attention. He spoke above everyone else and laughed uproariously, never allowing himself to be understated or demure. He acted as if life itself was a stage and he had a part to play.

We saw each other quite often at that barbershop, where I spent a lot of time hanging out with the men and women who worked there. I wore my hair in a pixie cut back then and would have it trimmed on the women's side of the shop and then tapered on the men's. My son, Naiim, was just two years old and received his first professional haircut at that shop. It was the kind of place where anyone could just hang out, whether being serviced or not, and it seemed as if I would run into Aeron once a week, every week, that summer.

Still, he never grew on me.

One evening, after the shop closed, a group of us left and went to a recording studio to continue hanging out. Once we arrived, it was easy to notice Aeron was already there, being his usual boisterous and annoying self, except it was all amplified, as he seemed to be under the influence of something—something that made him talk louder and faster than usual. After a few hours, Aeron fell asleep on a sofa in the building's common area, and I decided to play a prank on the attention-craving former child actor. As he slept, his hands dangling off the edge of the couch, and with a crowd of acquaintances watching and snickering, I took a bottle of Wite-Out I found atop a nearby desk and proceeded to paint Aeron's nails with the thick white liquid. The rest of the group burst out laughing and I couldn't help but laugh, too. By the time Aeron awoke, the Wite-Out was dry and none of us had any recommendations on how he could remove the paint from his nails.

"Man! Who did this shit?" he grumbled as he rose from the sofa, looking at his nails. No one answered; we all just laughed. Aeron looked at me. "Did you do this?"

"I didn't do shit!" I insisted as I grabbed my purse and headed out the door, fleeing the scene of the crime. It would be weeks later, back at the barbershop, before I admitted I was the culprit. To make up for the prank, I took an eight-by-ten, black-and-white photograph of myself from my car and scribbled upon it, *Sorry for getting white stuff all over your fingers.*

All was forgiven.

I'm sure I ran into Aeron several more times over the next seven years but each time I saw him, I could never recall when or where I saw him last. He just always seemed to be there. He was one of those people you'd see quite randomly about town and now here he was again. He was sitting in a barber's chair at Le Vie L'Orange, ironically enough, having his haircut, when I walked past him during my tour of the salon and spa.

"Hey, girl! How have you been? God, I haven't seen you in a minute!" he said, as our eyes met.

"I've seen you here and there, I'm sure, but one of the last times I remember seeing you was that time I painted your fingernails with Wite-Out," I answered, chuckling at the thought.

"That's right!" he exclaimed as he rose from the chair, his haircut complete. "I almost forgot about that! Man, do you know how hard it is to get Wite-Out off your nails? I had to walk around with that shit on my hands for damn near three weeks!"

I laughed so hard, my stomach ached, and I tried to issue a sincere apology through my cackle. "I am . . . so . . . sorry!"

Aeron reached into his pocket, pulled out a bottle of nasal spray, and squirted it into one nostril and then the next. I figured it was allergies. We struck up a conversation and for some reason after all those years, Aeron was attractive to me. He was tall and broad. He was strong and protective. He was tangible.

He wasn't thousands of miles away, like Wayne.

Over the next several hours, we drank and talked and laughed and Aeron continued to inhale his nasal spray until the bottle was empty. "Come with me," he insisted as he grabbed my hand and led me through the back door of the building. He walked me to his car, opened the driver's side door, and removed a small bag of white powder from the center console. With his teeth, he removed the tip of the nose spray bottle, shook the white powder into it, and added a bit of water from a bottle he stashed in his car, before resealing and shaking the inhalant.

"Gotta take my medicine," he said. He rubbed a bit of the white powder on his teeth before continuing. "Coke and a smile!"

The powder was cocaine and though this should have been the first red flag, I ignored his drug use and shrugged it off as a thing child stars do. After all, this is Hollywood! You can't swing a bat in this town without hitting a cokehead, and we've all heard the stories of the lives child actors live once they become adults and their careers become obscure. I supposed it was all par for the course and decided to ignore it and enjoy his company, nonetheless. I was delighted just to have a regular conversation with someone. It had been years since I'd been engaged in such a way, as I'd spent most of that time on tour, being interviewed, poked and prodded by the public. My life changed drastically after the publication of *Confessions of a Video Vixen* and I'd found solace in my home, nestled in the suburban hills, when not on the road. But, soon, that solace turned into an anxious confinement.

My home became my hermitage.

I also felt a bond with Aeron because he'd been the victim of vicious rumors and was quite the social outcast. And I felt like an outcast. He wasn't cool or trendy; he was awkward and dated, and I figured he and I were both outcasts in our own ways and he would understand what it was like to be attacked by people, as I had been attacked upon publishing *Confessions* in 2005. I figured, given his image in certain circles, he wouldn't be in any position to judge me. He may have been a Goody Two-shoes to the general public, but people in the entertainment industry who knew Aeron shared stories of his abuse of the women he dated and his crazy mother. Sure, I'd heard all the rumors, but there were so many rumors floating around about me that I was more attracted to him *because* of this. I thought I'd found someone who could understand me, who wouldn't attack me, someone who could relate to what I was going through at that stage of my life and career.

Old acquaintances and long-lost family members had been crawling out of the woodwork since *Confessions*, all wanting a piece of me.

There were people I thought were my friends who proved otherwise, and a failed relationship that ended early in 2007 left me unsure of myself for a while. I was constantly berated by the public and crucified by millions for living my life much the way men do—without apology or regret. I was being called every horrible thing you could call a woman, every single day. People I didn't know, all over the world, were throwing stones at me for simply telling the truth.

My truth.

I wasn't the first to report from the misogynistic world of popular music and entertainment, but I surely wasn't met with the celebratory awe that surrounded my predecessors like Pamela Des Barres, Cynthia Albritton, or even Devon Wilson—the black super groupie famous for her affairs with Mick Jagger, Jim Morrison, and Jimi Hendrix. But those were different times. In 2005, I became public enemy number one while also becoming more successful than some of the men and the vast majority of the general public who deemed me as such. So, I took the bad with the good and hoped to find someone who would accept it all and give me stability outside the limelight.

For all the wonderful things that were happening to me, there were gaping holes in my life that needed to be filled, and Aeron appeared at just the right time—or maybe it was the wrong time. I couldn't be sure. I'd been dating Wayne for just over six months and though I'd already fallen in love with him and had no intentions of leaving him, I had this incredible craving for normalcy, for my world to stop spinning. I went into my relationship with Wayne knowing I would always be one of many and that he and I would spend more time apart than together. I was lonely. I wanted someone local, someone reachable, someone normal with whom I could hole up when in Los Angeles. Aeron was the exact opposite of Wayne. He wasn't powerful, he wasn't rich, he wasn't a star, and by the end of the event at Le Vie L'Orange, he was massaging my feet and I was calling him my husband. The desperation was palpable and the foreshadowing was unfortunate.

By the time the sun began to set, the event was nearing its end and I decided it was time to go. Aeron walked me to my car, refusing to say good-bye, and instead asked me to dinner. "Do you want to go grab something to eat in a little bit?"

"Yeah, sure. Just let me run home and change," I suggested. I wore shorts and a spaghetti-strapped blouse that afternoon and wanted to wear something more appropriate for dinner and the chilly evening weather.

"That's fine. I need to close out the event, anyway." Aeron and his uncle were promoting the event as part of their new and soon failed event-planning venture. Aeron was always grasping at straws.

"Alright. So, I'll meet you in about an hour and have Jawn come with us, too," I suggested. Jawn and Aeron had known each other for years and I felt the need to have a buffer. Aeron was still the loud, hyper man I'd met years before, and after watching him spray cocaine into his nose, I wasn't sure how stable or unstable the rest of the night would be.

"Okay. Let's meet at Dan Tana's, then."

"Cool."

Aeron leaned over and kissed me tenderly on the left corner of my lips. Internally, I melted and swooned, while being outwardly nonchalant. I don't know what it was about him or about me that day, but something happened; something clicked. After finding him so obtuse from our very first encounter seven years before, he all of a sudden seemed right for me.

I didn't know if any of the rumors about him were true. Rumors run wild in the entertainment business. I didn't know much about him at all. But I guess it didn't matter what I knew about him. What mattered was what I knew about me. I was looking for something familiar, something from before my fame. I was looking for someone from those barbershop days before I had money, before I had anything. Maybe I needed a touchstone, something and someone to make me feel normal. Maybe I needed someone who would just be there—someone who, unlike Wayne, wasn't bigger than my life or me.

Whatever the reason, I ignored all the red flags. I kissed Aeron back and solidified our dinner plans for later, when what I should have done was left him right where I found him, as I always had before. It was that moment, that sliver of time right there, I wish I could take back. In that split second, I made the one decision that would change my life in ways no one could have predicted.

CHAPTER THREE

Thieves in the Temple

Aeron and I began dating right away. After dinner that night at Dan Tana's, he followed me home and stayed for nearly a week. We bared our souls those first few days, sharing our secrets and dispelling rumors, bonding over our one common denominator—bad reputations. He told me about doing drugs with an ex-girlfriend and going as a couple to be tested for STDs and HIV on her dead father's birthday. Her HIV test results were negative, while his initially showed up as positive. He told me about the panic that ensued and the dietary and supplemental regimen he started, hoping to ward off the virus if, in fact, he was infected. As is customary for patients who test positive for the deadly disease, he was made to take several more tests, each of them having negative results. It seemed his initial diagnosis was a false positive. But, just to be sure, in those first few days, we traveled to the drug store for an at-home HIV test, sent his blood sample off to the lab, and waited just forty-eight hours for his negative results. It was an intense few days—a soul-baring festival of full disclosure.

He was charming and attentive. He immediately took to taking care of the house and me. He spent those first few days worrying about me as I suffered through what I thought was a very bad cold, with which I'd been struggling for over a week. This was what I needed. Aeron came into my life at a vulnerable time when being sick and alone only magnified the things Wayne couldn't give me as he and his entourage traveled the country in a convoy of tour buses. Aeron was a real person and I needed a real person to take care of me.

But our little infirmary was soon disrupted.

Aeron was expecting a child with a young woman in Chicago, and in July, just a few days after we were reunited, she went into labor and Aeron was on his way to be with her and their newborn son. Ironically, on the same night he was scheduled to fly to Chicago, I was due to meet Wayne in Washington, D.C. So Aeron and I traveled to Los Angeles International Airport together and he stayed with me until my flight boarded, before boarding his. I was sad to leave Aeron but more excited to be on my way to see the man I loved. It seemed I was on the verge of having it all—an exciting life on the road with an artist on the brink of becoming an international superstar and a man at home to take care of me.

It all seemed so perfect.

I spent the next several days with Wayne, loving every moment but anxious to talk to him about my desire for normalcy. "I wish you were average," I said while sitting on his bus during a road trip. "I mean, I want to go to the grocery store and to Home Depot without causing a scene. I want to go to the movies like regular couples and walk around the mall. I can't do that with you. All we have is this bus and these hotel rooms, the road and all these people around us."

"I'm never going to be regular or average. I've never been those things, not one day of my life," Wayne rebutted.

"Then I don't know how long I can do this."

"You just let me know when you're ready to go."

"Okay." But there was no way I'd ever be ready to go. My heart was with Wayne and it meant nothing to me that Aeron was spending time with his brand-new baby and the child's mother. Well, not until I returned home a week later to an empty house, my cough and congestion plenty worse than it was when I left. I missed having Aeron with me, taking care of me, and I needed him then more than ever.

I was growing sicker by the day.

I urged him to hurry back every time he called to check in with me, and when he landed in Los Angeles two weeks after his departure, his first stop was my place. Instantly, Aeron fell back into his new role and began caring for me. He conjured up homemade elixirs and prepared hot baths for me with salts and oils to ease my congestion. Still, nothing worked. I drank Buckley's cough syrup straight from the bottle and guzzled a gallon of water a day, trying to ease my inflamed throat and painful cough.

Another week passed and I'd been sick for over four weeks when Aeron suggested I may have bronchitis and we should rush to the emergency room. But all I heard was that I needed to go to the hospital—that *I* needed to go. There was no *we* in my vocabulary. I had grown so accustomed to being on my own and doing everything for myself since I was a teenager that I just got dressed and walked out the front door, announcing, "I'll be right back!"

Startled, Aeron followed me through the door and down the driveway as I hopped into my SUV. "Do you want me to go with you?" he asked, concerned.

"Nah. I'm good. I'll be right back," I insisted before kissing him and backing through the opened gates of my property.

Aeron just stood there and watched me drive off. A few minutes later, he called me to reiterate, "I really wish you would have let me come with you. I mean, who drives themselves to the emergency room if they don't have to?"

"I do. I'm just accustomed to doing everything alone. It's not a big deal. I'll be back in a couple hours. I'll text you and let you know how things are going."

"Okay."

That's just the sort of woman I'd become. I was used to being in the world alone and doing things on my own. I ran away from my father's house when I was just sixteen and had been a single mother since nineteen. I made a way for myself in the world against incredible odds and I was not in the habit of depending on anyone for anything. I hustled my way through life and created lanes where there were none.

But there was always just one thing missing—one *big* thing—family.

I was born into a broken family, to a mother who could never be one and a father who was busy starting new families everywhere he decided to call home. My mother was a shell and my father was a ghost.

And I was their daughter.

As I got older and people started moving away, there were no aunts or uncles, no grandparents, no cousins—there were no connections. There was all this blood between us, and even though we could all be linked to one another by that blood, it was never enough to bind us.

So there I was, a single mother with no family, no ties. My son, Naiim, was nine years old and had never known a father, grandfather, or uncle. I wanted someone for him. I wanted someone for me. And as the emergency room doctor confirmed that I, in fact, had chronic bronchitis, my wanting instantly turned into a need. I was very, very sick and there was a man waiting at home, begging to do nothing but care for me. So, I left the emergency room and sped back to him.

Over the next several weeks, I continued to suffer with chronic bronchitis, grateful to have Aeron with me on the nights I awoke startled and unable to breathe, fearing the need for CPR. It was the scariest time in my life; I struggled with everyday things, my lungs giving out on me often. I was more vulnerable than I'd ever been. Aeron was staying over most every night, leaving in the morning to go about his usual affairs but checking on me many times during the day. Any time I called and said I needed him, he would stop what he was doing and rush right over. He cooked and cleaned and got to know my son. He fixed things around the house and made sure

I needed for nothing while sick and recovering. It seemed I'd made the right choice when I chose him, as did he, when he chose me.

Still, it wasn't my intention to stop or change my life for him. Behind his back, when talking to my girlfriends, I referred to him as my new houseboy. He did everything that needed to be done around the house and that suited me just fine when I wasn't with Wayne. Aeron was a new father to a little boy named Jonah, and the drama that ensued between him and Jonah's mother soon after Jonah's birth was of no interest to me. I didn't need Aeron to be my everything; I just needed him to play house with me in between my road trips with Wayne. I wanted to eat my cake and have it, too. I wanted all my emotional gaps filled and I wanted to live wild and free with my road warrior lover.

I wanted it all and I had it all—for a time.

After visiting the emergency room three times a week, every week, for a few months, I was finally getting over my bout with chronic bronchitis. Aeron and I were still spending plenty of time together, but I didn't need him there as much and he was able to resume his regular schedule, though he found it difficult to do. We had already woven ourselves into one another and created a fabric all our own, blocking out most of the world. Still, I enjoyed my time alone just as much as I enjoyed our time together and reveled in my *eat the cake and have it* lifestyle. Then, one day, I received a call that rocked my security.

There was nothing unusual about my accountant calling me in the middle of the day, so I answered the phone gleefully, hoping for good news. "Hey, Samuel! What's up?"

"I just got a call from a detective at the Van Nuys Police Department who says he has your license plates, which he took off of a guy he arrested in your neighborhood several days ago."

My heart pounded. "What?"

"Go check your Mercedes. Do you have your plates?"

"I got them in the mail a few weeks ago and haven't put them on yet, since I haven't been driving that car. I stuck it between the driver's seat and the console," I explained as I rushed into my garage and opened the Mercedes' driver's side door. I looked in the crevice where I'd shoved them. "They're gone."

"Well, here's the number for the detective. Give him a call; he'll bring you the plates and explain what happened. I'm sure he'll have you make a statement, as well."

I hurried off the phone and, hands shaking, called the detective. Within the hour he was at my house, explaining how some wayward drifter broke into my garage through a side door three days prior, opened my unlocked car, and stole my plates. I recalled that day and how I'd just come home from picking up my son from school, leaving my gate open after driving into the garage since I didn't plan on being home more than an hour. I hurried into the house with Naiim before hopping in and out of the shower, dressing, and driving out again. I didn't engage the house's alarm that day. Based on what the detective told me, the thief must have been in my garage while I was home alone with my son, while I was showering and dressing. As he continued to demonstrate how close my son and I came to danger, the detective showed me the thief's mug shot and criminal arrest record, filled with assaults, rapes, and thefts.

I shuddered.

There I was, perched upon my safe hill, in my million-dollar home surrounded by other million-dollar homes, in this upstanding neighborhood, hiding from the world and all its dangers, and this man, this dangerous stranger, watched me come home, broke into my garage, and stole from me. It could have been so much worse, according to his rap sheet, and the thought of that propelled me to call Aeron.

"Hey, baby!" he answered, happy to hear from me.

I sobbed, "Baby, can you come over?"

"What's wrong? What happened?"

"Someone broke into the garage while I was home alone with Naiim. I was in the shower! He could have come into the house and I wouldn't have known! He was arrested for assaults and rapes and he could have done that to me!" I explained, unable to control my wails. "Can you move in? Can you just stay here with me?"

"You want me to move in?" he reaffirmed.

"Yeah. Please! I don't want to be alone anymore. I'm so scared!"

"I'm on my way."

And that was it.

It was August 2007 and in just one month's time, I had managed to complicate my life further. It's amazing what one bad decision can do and how, often, it's not the thieves who break in that pose the biggest threat, but the ones we invite inside.

CHAPTER FOUR

Breathe

I'd come to know Aeron as a kind, gentle man with a propensity to love and comfort. We were quite the couple by the time Aeron moved in, and he'd already brought me home to meet his mother, brother, sister, and extended family. Though it was my first time meeting his family, it wasn't my first time hearing about them. Aeron and I had a few mutual friends who had told stories about Aeron and his family in passing and who warned me about them once he and I began dating. Word around town and in the entertainment industry was that his mother was crazy and that he was a "mama's boy."

It didn't take long for me to find both rumors to be factual.

His mother, Mona, was nice enough upon meeting me and she did a very good job at befriending me, quickly. His sister, Samantha, and brother, Jonathan, were darling, calm spirits and the complete opposite of their erratic, spotlight-craving brother. I adored both of them, as well as their significant others. Jonathan's girlfriend and mother of his child wasted no time, however, pulling me aside to affirm all the wacky stories I'd heard about Aeron's mother and his emotionally incestuous relationship with her. When Aeron's father left the family over twenty years before, Aeron became the man of the house. As his mother's eldest son, as well as an impressive bread-winner since his first film role at the age of nine, Aeron replaced his father in the home and in his mother's heart. Soon, I would realize I wasn't just his girlfriend—I was his mother's competition.

As the end of August approached, Aeron and I had only been together just shy of two months, but in that short amount of time so much happened. We battled my chronic bronchitis, Jonah was born, and we were pushed together by an intruder. I continued to carry on a relationship with Wayne, finding it impossible to give up one for the other. So I juggled my love affair with the rapper along with my new family life in Los Angeles while helping to care financially for Aeron's newborn son, Jonah, in Chicago, sending money and boxes of supplies often. Aeron wasn't much of an earner, his acting career having hit a slump; therefore his responsibilities would have to become my responsibilities if I wanted to keep him in my life and close to me.

In a nutshell, I had to pay him to stay.

I didn't want Aeron away from me for too long. I grew accustomed to having him around the house, and in no time, my houseboy became my boyfriend and we were making plans for the future. Now I didn't have to be alone on birthdays and holidays. I had someone with whom I could share my *actual* life, someone with whom I could be normal and forget all the fame and privilege I'd acquired in the couple of years since *Confessions of a Video Vixen* was published. I was creating a bubble in which to live and Aeron was a big part of it; I was willing to do whatever it took to keep that bubble from bursting.

So, I paid off Aeron's smaller debts and gave him money and supplies to send to Chicago. If Mona needed money, I gave it to him to give to her. It felt like I was supporting everything and everyone around me, all in hopes of keeping my bubble intact—all in hopes of being normal and creating the family I never had. With me, Aeron needed for nothing. He lived in a million-dollar house on a hill with access to my cars and my money. There was a maid, a pool man, and a gardener to take care of the grounds, and there was me—always making him feel loved. All he had to do was stay good. But soon the real Aeron would rear up and show himself to be far uglier than his clean-cut, church-boy public image or at-home caregiver persona. There was a dark, evil man living inside of him and it would only take a conversation about Wayne to bring it out.

Aeron and I made plans to spend the night of August 24 celebrating my twenty-ninth birthday. We enjoyed dinner at Yamashiro, a legendary Japanese restaurant high in the Hollywood Hills. The night was a perfect mixture of laughter, kisses, and sake. It was going so well, I tipped the bathroom attendant one hundred dollars on the way out of the restroom. I was happy. After finishing dinner and drinks, we motioned for the valet to bring Aeron's car. As we waited, we walked through the Japanese garden just in front of the restaurant, which overlooked all of Hollywood and Los Angeles. The night air was chilly so Aeron wrapped me in his jacket and his large, strong, manly arms.

This was normalcy and safety at its best.

We were on our way to the W Hotel in Westwood, a suburb of West Los Angeles, when Aeron received a call from his brother, Jonathan, who was working as a security guard at a strip club on the unsavory east side of town. Aeron asked if I minded making a detour. The night was going so well, I saw no reason to protest. So we hopped into Aeron's car and made the fifteen-minute drive to the east side to meet his brother. When we arrived, Jonathan greeted us, showed us to a booth in the nearly empty club, and sat with us.

Soon, and for whatever reason, the conversation turned to music. Aeron began to bash Wayne and his work, already fully aware of my relationship with the superstar rapper. Aeron was part of a musical family, each and every one of them talented but none of them successful. He played local dives and had been in the studio since I met him back in 2000, trying to break into the music industry and become a recording star. He hated being referred to as an actor, even though acting had always been his bread and butter.

Basically, Aeron was jealous of Wayne, not just because of his success in the music industry but because of his relationship with me.

As hard as he tried to steal me away from Wayne, there was nothing he could do, and as much as I wanted to be a part of this normal couple and this bullshit normal conversation where the have-nots hate on those who have accomplished more than they ever would in their lifetimes, I couldn't sit by and let anyone talk badly about my love. No matter what, I was still in love with Wayne, and more than that, I respected and revered him. Jonathan defied Aeron, making it clear that he was a fan of Wayne and his music—as did I. However, my protest was taken more harshly.

"That noise Lil' Wayne is making is not real music. That shit is garbage. That man can't even play an instrument but he's calling himself a musician!"

"Actually, he *does* play an instrument and it doesn't matter whether you think he's a musician or not; he sells more records than you'll ever sell with that old-head music you like to make. Nobody's listening to that shit you create. It's a new millennium. Get into it." As a struggling musician, Aeron was desperate to be appreciated and admired as an artist by the world and by me, his girl.

But I never could.

Aeron rose from the table in a huff, walked away, and stood alongside the stage as a stripper danced for him. He peeled a few one-dollar bills from a very small stack and tossed them her way. One dollar. Two dollars. Three dollars, four. It was laughable. I was accustomed to big money—mine and those of my associates—and looking at his pathetic ploy to seem like a big fish only made me want to show him just how small he really was. I was reeling from his comments about Wayne and thought he had no place and no right to talk about him that way. I was angry and grew even angrier as I watched him pretend to be some sort of big shot, draping five one-dollar bills in the G-string of a busted stripper in an empty club in East Los Angeles. I wanted him to know he was nothing.

I wanted him to know he wasn't Wayne.

So, intoxicated, I walked over, slapped him as hard as I could, and stormed out.

Aeron followed closely behind as I walked out to the abandoned parking lot, Jonathan trailing behind us. As I walked toward his car, Aeron wrapped those same big, strong, manly arms that had once warmed me around my neck, placing me in a chokehold and squeezing like a boa constrictor.

I gasped for air. I clawed at his arms, face, and neck.

"I can't breathe," I whispered, nearly lifeless.

"Go to sleep, bitch," Aeron chanted, over and over, until I passed out and fell to the ground, splitting my lip and gashing the side of my face. Jonathan urged him to stop but did nothing more.

An employee of the club called the police and after just a minute of unconsciousness, I came to, alone and on the pavement in the parking lot. The world spun as I gasped for breath, my pink shirt red with blood. Aeron was long gone and I knew where he was headed—my place. I scrambled to find my phone inside my purse, called a cab, and left before the police arrived.

I begged the driver to get to my address as soon as he could, hoping to beat Aeron there and secure the house before he could get in, but as the cab pulled up to my house, Aeron was already speeding off. I rushed inside to find he'd taken all of his things, relieved he took nothing of mine. Battered, bruised, and bleeding, I slid down the wall of my bathroom, crying. Anyone with self-respect would have known this was the end and would have cut their losses and moved on.

Anyone with self-respect.

CHAPTER FIVE

Overjoyed

adly bruised, cut, and bleeding from my face, I finally
called the police. Within the hour, two officers arrived
to take a battery and injury report along with photos as
evidence of the attack. I also called Mona to let her know what her
son had done and she hurried over, supposedly to support me. The
truth was, she was there to keep an eye on what was going on and
what all of this meant for her son. She sat at my breakfast nook as
the police questioned me and took pictures. She sat there on her
phone and it never dawned on me that she was, most likely, sitting
there calling an attorney to defend him and repeating everything
being said between the police and me. Naive and hopeful, I never
thought that, as a woman, she would not be on my side but on her
son's—no matter how wrong he was.

Later that night, after everyone left, I reached out to Wayne to
tell him what had happened, hoping he would insist I board the first
plane headed to Miami, where he lived. He was always there when I
needed him and never said no when I wanted to see him. No matter
what, we always found a way to be together as often as we could.
Tearfully, I explained to Wayne all that had happened as he stayed

on the phone, silent. It didn't dawn on me this was his first time hearing about Aeron and, instead of being angered by the abuse, he fixated on the fact that I had a boyfriend who was living with me.

I wanted to go to him. I wanted to get out of that place, out of my relationship with Aeron, abandon this idea of having a normal family, and just be with Wayne.

"You chose him, you deal with him," Wayne said, before hanging up.

And that was it.

I sat on the floor in my bathroom that night and cried. I called Wayne over and over again, and eventually he just turned his phone off, sending all my calls to voicemail. I wanted him to save me. I needed a lifeline and he was everything to me—my only hope. After all, I had been defending *his* honor and I could have died doing so. But Wayne couldn't hear any of that; he didn't hear me crying, pleading for him. I needed him that night; I needed him to save me from myself, from this idea of normalcy, and the monster I thought could deliver it. I needed him to forgive me for wanting what I thought was more and give me a reason to never go back. Instead, he gave me silence. He wouldn't answer my calls for the next month.

I was devastated.

As the severity of the situation between Aeron and me sank in, Aeron and his mother did everything they could to sweep it under the rug. I was so vulnerable, so alone, so broken, and with nowhere to go, I melted when Mona said, "We're a family and family sticks together." So, within a few days, Aeron, Mona, Naiim, and I were on our way to Santa Barbara to continue my birthday celebration as planned and as a family. I covered my cuts and bruises with makeup, smeared lipstick on my busted lip, and we piled into the Range Rover and took the two-hour drive, acting as if the incident never happened. In Santa Barbara we spent several days at the Bacara Resort and Spa, a trip that I funded. I paid for everyone to stay and eat and have a lovely time as I kept checking my compact mirror to be sure my makeup was still concealing my bruises and open wounds.

But I wasn't fooling anyone.

Despite all my efforts to make everyone happy and to be a part of this family Mona insisted we were, she complained the entire trip. Nothing at the renowned, four-star resort was good enough for her. Every crack in the sidewalk, every scratch in the silverware, was fodder for her discontent. But it wasn't the award-winning, beach-front accommodations that weren't good enough for her; it was me. She was jealous that I was able to take care of her son in ways she couldn't, and no matter what I did, no matter the cuts and bruises on my face and body, *I* was the one who wasn't good enough for *him*. No one could ever be—no one but Mona. I was taking abuse from the son and the mother, and I was, literally, paying for it.

In stark contrast to his mother, Aeron was delightful during our trip as he did his best to sugarcoat the issues and lull me into an emotional sleep. If I'd wanted to, I had everything I needed to make him pay for what he did to me, to ruin his life and whatever career he had left. With my battered face, I was the powerful one, but it never felt that way. I was too overcome with defeat to realize I could change everything, put this abusive monster away in a prison cell, and stop him from ever harming another woman.

I loved Aeron with a gross display of what I would later describe as Relationship Stockholm—a term I coined in my third book as a play on Stockholm Syndrome, a psychological condition wherein captives express empathy and even love for their captors, defending them despite the pain these captors inflict. Victims often mistake a lack of or lapse in abuse as a show of kindness in this form of traumatic bonding. Stockholm Syndrome describes *"strong emotional ties that develop between two persons where one person intermittently harasses, beats, threatens, abuses, or intimidates the other."* These definitions describe my relationship with Aeron, precisely.

But I didn't know that, then.

All I knew was I was relieved and grateful for Aeron's tenderness during the trip, taking it as an act of kindness that he wasn't hitting or choking me. As we danced our first dance to Stevie Wonder's "Overjoyed," in front of a crowd of complete strangers, I buried my head in his chest, hiding my battered face from onlookers. I'd never danced with a man before and was unsure of where my feet should go. Aeron led me. I followed. I would follow him anywhere. As the band played the music, Aeron sang the lyrics and I cried silently into his chest.

After our trip to Santa Barbara, I hesitated to file charges against Aeron—but I didn't have to because the state of California had already done so. By the time those charges were filed and we were scheduled to meet the City Attorney, it was November and I was in deep over my head. Aeron and his mother hired famed celebrity defender Shawn Chapman Holley, most recently known for her role in the defense of Lindsey Lohan, to represent him. Aeron drove us downtown for the meeting and we walked into the City Attorney's office hand in hand, a united front. When I think back on it, it's so hard to make sense of it all. But we were a family; we were sticking together.

I was missing something—I'd always been missing something.

I was always alone in the world with no connections and no family, no one to defend me or be there when I needed help or got into trouble. I'd been fending for myself since I was sixteen years old and men had been hitting me since my junior high school boyfriend slapped me at the bus stop one morning before school. Everything I learned about life was violent. By the time I was thirteen, I'd been beaten, kidnapped, raped, and held at gunpoint.

My mother beat me. She taught me the language of violence from a very young age. She was the first to draw blood from my face. So why would it seem strange when someone else did? Aeron was speaking the same language and no matter how damaging it was to my spirit, it was the only language I'd ever been taught.

I understood it.

Like millions of other abused women and sufferers of Stockholm Syndrome and its related illnesses, I was protecting my abuser. So, after telling the City Attorney I was too drunk to recall the incident in order to save Aeron from prison time for applying what the authorities called a felony choke hold, we sat outside the office for a legal wrap-up of the situation. Shawn Chapman Holley warned us about our behavior and reminded Aeron of how close he'd come to being in very serious legal trouble.

As she lectured us about *our* behavior, I unwrapped the scarf I wore around my neck to reveal recent bruises from when Aeron had choked me again, just a few days before. "It's not *our* behavior! It's *his* behavior! I didn't do this to myself!" I blurted.

"Aeron," she said, looking at my bruised neck, "it would be a good idea for you to have her sign a confidentiality agreement so that none of this gets out."

Everyone was protecting Aeron. Even me.

Well, if I knew nothing else, I knew that one day I would need to tell my story, even and especially if it meant saving my life, and there was no way I would agree to a confidentiality agreement. The topic never came up again and the abuse continued through the next year, even after Jonah came to live with us. Aeron and I would tell everyone the baby was mine as he was ashamed to have a child outside of a committed relationship and with a woman he barely knew and didn't love. He was always concerned with upholding his church-boy image with the general public. He somehow convinced the child's mother to hand over the baby in exchange for several thousand dollars, making her sign a custody agreement giving him sole, legal custody. She was young and dumb and whatever the dollar amount, it was a lot for a young girl living on the South Side of Chicago. She was already the mother of a young daughter whose father was unknown and they were living on welfare. I figured she must have thought Aeron was the best thing that could have happened to her life at the time. But I figured her life was just as ruined as mine.

Just over a year old, Jonah quickly took to calling me *mom* and my longing for a family was satisfied while my ability to protect myself against abuse continued to falter. The beatings and choking were frequent and the mental and emotional abuse raged. The police were called to our home eight or nine times between 2007 and 2009, and the neighbors were well aware of our tumultuous relationship. I was too embarrassed to meet their eyes, so I would drop my head and turn my back whenever confronted with a friendly hello. As introverted as I was before my relationship with Aeron, I became even more so as the relationship became increasingly abusive. I was ashamed yet steadfast in my decision to stay with him and make it work, hoping that one day it would get better.

It didn't.

Aeron would disappear for days, weeks, and even months at a time, taking Jonah with him. He would seldom call home and when he did pop up, it would only be for sex or food, money, maybe a nap and a shower, before leaving again. I tried everything I could to hold our family together, failing at the task and at life. By 2008 I was a shell of who I was the year before, broken by Aeron's actions and treatment of me. My independence was shattered and whatever form of esteem I mustered due to my professional accomplishments waned. I was completely and hopelessly wrapped up into my relationship with Aeron, and I was going to have the family I always wanted—even if it killed me.

It was around this time I came across a video on the Internet of Aeron on a date with two women. The threesome had apparently attended the premiere of Tyler Perry's film *Why Did I Get Married*, in October 2007, only two months after he'd moved in, while I was on tour for my second book, *The Vixen Diaries*. I watched the video in disgust to see Aeron holding hands with one woman and grabbing the other around her waist as they trotted into the event. I fumed. While I was away, promoting the book and the career that fed him and his child and kept them clothed, in the nicest cars, and in a million-dollar home, Aeron was out cruising the streets of Los Angeles with not one, but *two* dates.

I was humiliated.

Aeron and I had managed to keep the abusive nature of our relationship a secret from the public during our first year together, but this was a gross and public display of his disregard for the family I thought we had built. And for me, it was the first public sign that my bubble was compromised.

CHAPTER SIX

Rings and Things

Though the movie premiere had taken place more than six months prior to my finding the video, Aeron had never brought it to my attention—he'd never once mentioned dropping my son off at his friend's house and taking two women on a date. Of course not. His disrespect was blatant and public and my complacency was stifling. Throughout my relationship with Aeron, he always knew about my ongoing dealings with Wayne and accepted it. I was always honest with him about Wayne and never tried to hide my relationship with him. That was one of the reasons I thought Aeron was right for me; he didn't seem to want to change me. Everyone knew about my relationship with Wayne, as it made for interesting magazine copy. Wayne and I spoke about our love affair often in interviews and made no efforts to hide it when traveling together. Even though Aeron professed to be advanced enough to stomach being the under-achieving boyfriend to a successful woman with an ultrasuccessful lover, obviously he wasn't as equipped as he claimed.

I called Aeron and confronted him with the information. "Why am I looking at footage of you and two women going to this premiere while I was on tour last year?"

"I don't know what you're talking about," he huffed.

"The *Why Did I Get Married* premiere! And where was my son?"

"I took him to my friend's house! What the fuck is the problem?"

"What friend? Where? We didn't have a conversation about any of this! Why would you drop my kid off at some random person's house!"

"It wasn't a random person, it was my friend, and I shouldn't have to call you and get your permission about what to do with Naiim when he's in my care!"

The truth was, our relationship was a power struggle.

Aeron resented everything about me, especially my authority. I was the breadwinner. Around the house, all decisions had to go through me and he couldn't stand not being in control or feeling like a man. He was a loser and a has-been and my success only irritated him by reiterating that. He wished *he* were the one on tour, being paid to do what he loved. He resented my growing recognition and never missed an opportunity to ruin any positive experience in my life and career. This incident, taking two women out on a date while I was on tour, was no different. For me, a man who couldn't be relied upon to pay his fair share of household expenses could never be the head. He would never be a man to me. A man just doesn't seem to be a man when there is a woman taking care of him. Subconsciously, he would always be my houseboy, the guy who cooked and cleaned and unclogged the drains. In the beginning, Aeron showed me he was okay with this role and was very good at it, but now, with his true demeanor on display, he was rebelling against this role and against me.

The only way Aeron could fight against his inability to gain or earn my respect was to use his fists. He exacted his strength through the use of brute force and bullying. He needed to belittle and diminish me at every turn in order to make himself feel authoritative. He tapped into my fear, unable to earn my respect, and it was upon that fear that our entire relationship was based. Wayne offered me one thing, but Aeron knew the concept and public appearance of having a family outweighed being one of many lovers to some rapper. So, he dangled the possibility of having a functioning family just out of my reach and I was always chasing it.

After confronting him with the video proof, Aeron didn't come home that night or any night that week. Incidences like this, especially those involving other women, were plenty—too many to recount as the tug-of-war between us waged on.

My nerves were wrecked.

Since being diagnosed with Generalized Anxiety Disorder back in 2006, I had learned to control my nervous condition with prescription drugs, namely Xanax. Eventually, I hoped to wean myself off the drug completely and rely only on breathing and mind-over-matter techniques. I didn't take the medication often, at first. I used it only during uncontrollable panic attacks and unnerving situations like traveling. A thirty-day supply would last me ninety days or more.

But that was before Aeron.

Now, with the constant abuse and abandonment and with my desperate need to make this mess into a functioning, normal family, I began taking the Xanax to keep sane, washing them down with alcohol. I would begin my mornings with a pill and a couple beers and every two hours, the same, from morning until night. I sat in my office, writing, and went about my daily household responsibilities, subdued. I was doing the best I could to remain calm, rational, and focused while meeting my contractual obligations to my publisher and trying not to argue with Aeron about whichever woman he was seeing or the number of days he'd gone missing that week. I just didn't want to make things worse, so I self-medicated often.

It didn't take long for a serious drug and alcohol addiction to form. My thirty-day supplies were lasting just over a week, so I began buying the drug from street dealers. But Aeron never noticed. He was never present, and now, neither was I. I dropped weight at an alarming rate and often went a full week without eating or drinking anything except alcohol. I turned down invitations to award shows, parties, and events and even missed a portion of my book tour, to my publisher's horror, because of the issues at home and my ghastly physical condition.

My life was unraveling and I didn't know how to stop the fray.

Aeron was constantly making promises he had no intention of keeping, disappointing me over and over again. But Aeron and I weren't the only ones in this relationship. My son, Naiim, was always watching and he was seeing his mother deteriorate right before his eyes. When I was sad, he was sad, and though I tried to comfort him and reassure him that everything was okay, he knew nothing was. Still, he tried to make it work because I tried to make it work, and every time Aeron came home, Naiim would enjoy their brief times together. He would look forward to the visits, which they called Man Time, an experience that, since there were no other men in his life, Naiim never had before. In retrospect, I gave my son my disease. He was growing accustomed to the abuse I was taking, but also longed for a sense of family and counted his time with Aeron as acts of kindness.

So, one day in mid-2008, when Aeron called and promised Naiim he'd be home that night for some much-needed Man Time, my son prepared by setting up his gaming console and sitting on the edge of his bed—waiting. Hours passed. I called Aeron to see what was keeping him but he ignored my calls and subsequent text messages. It was after 10 PM when my son finally gave up waiting, turned off his bedroom lights, and crawled under the covers. I tucked him in and tried to make light of the situation, explaining that Aeron was caught up at work and would make it up to him. Naiim nodded his head and closed his eyes. I walked out of my son's room, heartbroken, plopped into my bed, and began texting Aeron, again. From the other side of the wall, I heard my son wailing.

His heart was broken, too.

I ran into his room, scooped my son from his mattress, and held him, crying with him. "I'm so sorry, baby. I'm so sorry I did this to you," I mumbled through my tears. Watching my son fall apart was the last straw for me, that day. I held him until he fell asleep, laid him back onto his pillow, and tiptoed out of his room, closing the door behind me. I knew where Aeron was; he was just a few minutes down the road at a recording studio, trying to live out his dream of being a recording star and failing horribly at it. Though his love of music was genuine, recording was a hobby that garnered him no income and I begged him to treat it as such—to stop putting music before everything else in his life, especially his family.

He hadn't been home in weeks and made a habit of leaving Jonah with his mother or sister or even taking the small child to studio sessions. A recording studio without drugs and alcohol is hard to imagine. He was only concerned with himself, and now the full weight of that and of my unfortunate decision to be with him was more evident to me than ever. I got dressed, grabbed my car keys, and headed to the recording studio to confront Aeron—and retrieve the twenty-five-thousand-dollar sapphire and diamond ring I'd given him. At this stage in our relationship, we were already calling one another husband and wife and I bought the rings to match the fantasy. Naturally, he took the jewels seriously but not the relationship.

Eight minutes later, I pulled into the driveway of the studio. There was a man standing outside the building, talking on the phone. As he saw me pull up, he ran inside to fetch Aeron. A few moments later, Aeron emerged and walked right past my car and toward his, which was parked tandem with a wall in front of it and another vehicle behind it.

"Give me back my ring, Aeron!" I yelled as I hopped out of my SUV and headed toward him. "Naiim waited for you all fucking day and you didn't show up for him!"

"I'm working, Karrine. Leave me alone!" he shouted back, as he unlocked his car door and slipped into the driver's seat.

"Give me back my ring, Aeron! We are over!"

"Fuck you! I'm not giving you shit!" Aeron closed the car door and started his car. I stood behind the vehicle, my arms folded, preventing him from backing up far enough to pull out. I was determined to retrieve the pricey ring before leaving the studio and Aeron. "Move!" he yelled out the window.

"I just want the ring! Give me my fucking ring!" I stood there in defiance as Aeron put his car in reverse and began inching back, threatening to pin me between his back bumper and the front bumper of the car behind his. I banged on the trunk of his car. "Stop! Stop! Just give me the ring, Aeron!"

A man came out from inside the studio and jumped into the car behind me, pulling out of the driveway and into the usually busy street just beyond it, before driving off. It was obvious Aeron had called him out to remove the car so he could make his escape. With the other vehicle gone, Aeron mashed on the gas and then the brake, over and over again. I banged on the trunk of the car, begging him to stop backing up and hand me the ring. But, still, he refused to do either. I took steps backward toward the street as he continued to back up, watching behind me as cars flew by the building. With one last mash of the gas, Aeron's car pushed me backward, just inches from the curb and a car speeding by. Instinctively, I hopped out of the road and onto the back bumper and hood of Aeron's car in order to not be hit by a passing vehicle. Aeron continued to back up into the street as I pounded on the trunk, begging him to pull back in and out of traffic. He refused. So, as I looked behind me and saw oncoming cars temporarily halted by a nearby stoplight, I hopped off and continued screaming at Aeron for my ring. He continued to ignore me, put his car in drive, and sped off, running over my foot.

And, with that, Aeron was gone.

A few days after the incident at the recording studio, police officers came to my home to serve me with a court summons. Aeron was petitioning for a restraining order against me. After everything he did to me—after the beatings and choking, after the times he literally hawked spit into my face, called me horrible names, after he degraded me, hurt my son, and *after* I saved his ass with the City Attorney, this is what he did.

But I didn't care.

I was happy to accept the summons and just as happy to not show up in court to dignify yet another attempt on his part to make me look like the bad or crazy one. Over the span of our relationship, while living with me, happily spending my money, brutally beating me, and emotionally damaging my son and me, Aeron never missed an opportunity to tell anyone who would listen what a horrible person I was. Several times, I received phone calls from magazine editors wanting my side of the story after Aeron took part in an interview, bashing me—all while still living with me. When confronted, Aeron always claimed to be misquoted or coerced in some way. He wasn't one to take responsibility for anything he did. It became obvious to me that Aeron was as focused on ruining me publicly as he was on doing so privately.

It was around this time that I requested copies of the injury report from my birthday in 2007, the night he choked me unconscious, as well as the photographic evidence of the attack. After being given the runaround when calling the Van Nuys police department, I was finally allowed instructions on how to gain access to the files, which had been moved to another precinct for some unexplained reason. Then, once I got my hands on the report, I was told that the Polaroid photos of my bloody face and injured body had been destroyed just thirty days after the incident. Though the injury report, with its diagram of my wounds, cuts, and scratches, was enough evidence, the photos from that night, the imagery of my battered face and bruised neck, would have been so much stronger. I wanted to have all the proof possible and to one day be able to show someone what Aeron had been doing to me. Alas, the report was all that was left and it would just have to be good enough.

Everywhere I went, people were protecting Aeron and I was being blamed for the abuse I endured—just as he wanted. He resented everything about me and would have killed me before he would have ever sung my praises or let anyone else do so. He clung desperately to his church-boy persona and deflected his deviance onto me. The world never heard about the things I learned about Aeron over the years, as I remained silent. But everyone heard from him as he berated me in public, beat me in private, and continued using me and depleting my finances.

Broken, I stayed through it all.

But something happened to me that night, the night I saw my son cry. I didn't love myself enough to leave Aeron, and over time my incessant need to be part of a family, any family, wore on my son as much as it did on me. Finally, I reached the end of my tether for the time being and was relieved to see Aeron go. God knows I would have never left him; he had to be the one who walked away from our tumultuous, abusive relationship. But when he did, I had no issues with moving forward quickly.

It took exactly seven days for me to begin dating someone else, and though he was nothing like Aeron, the new man in my life would be very similar to Wayne. In fact, they were more than similar; they were friends.

CHAPTER SEVEN

And He Held Me

Over the last several months before the demise of my relationship with Aeron, my relationship with Wayne had begun to, well, wane. After making my declaration that I wanted to be with a man more average and after he found out I was living with someone, we began to slowly drift apart. Things were just never the same. Then, as Wayne reveled in the super success of his June 2008 release, *Tha Carter III*, and all the attention it garnered him, our relationship seemed to have been stretched to its limits. It seemed we were finally over. Our phone conversations and text messages were fewer and farther between and when we did speak, it was forced and brief. We saw one another less frequently and soon, not at all.

Months before, around the time Wayne first started being aloof, I traveled to Atlanta for business, taking a red-eye flight from Los Angeles International Airport. Sitting behind me was Shad "Bow Wow" Moss. We didn't speak during the flight or during the tram ride to the baggage claim area once we landed in Atlanta. But we noticed each other. Though Wayne and I were in and out of contact at the time, I knew he and Shad were close friends, so I didn't dare make eye contact or invite conversation. I kept my eyes forward and ignored Shad, but I never forgot him.

So, in June, when an acquaintance named Reese mentioned she'd been involved with Shad, my ears perked. She described how they met and their sexual escapades and that now, he was being dismissive. With Wayne long gone and Aeron out of the picture, I was ready to move on and fast. On top of that, I can't pretend that getting involved with someone so close to Wayne didn't thrill me. I wanted to find a way to get his attention and get back at him for abandoning me. I wanted him to get angry, to get jealous, and to see me moving on within such close proximity with someone who was far from a loser—with someone he called *brother*.

I calculated my next moves.

"I can't believe what a dick Bow Wow is!" Reese proclaimed.

"Yeah, he sounds like a real fucking douche. Someone needs to teach him a lesson and give him a taste of his own medicine," I slyly suggested.

"Yes! Exactly!"

"He's a fucking kid. He needs a grown woman to put him in his place!"

"I wish you could do that for me."

"Do what?"

"Put him in his place."

"I'd love to but you have to be sure this is what you want because he may not want to be friends with you after I let him have it on your behalf."

"I don't care. Fuck him!"

"Okay. What's his number?" And just like that, I had him. I had no intention of calling Shad on her behalf—I barely knew her. I just needed a way in, a way to get closer to Shad and, eventually, closer to Wayne. As she read the number to me, I jotted it down, smirking on the other end of the phone. If this wasn't the oldest trick in the book, it should have been.

"Call him on three-way," she insisted. "He'll answer your number but not mine. He's been ignoring all my calls."

"I don't want to ambush him. Let me call him on my own and I'll call you back and tell you what happens. Stay by the phone."

"Okay. Cool."

It was like taking candy from a baby—a very big, very stupid baby. I ended my conversation with Reese and called Shad right away. It might be unusual for one person to call another if they've never met before, but I had a feeling he would forgive the intrusion.

"Hello?" he answered.

"Bow, it's Karrine Steffans," I said as I introduced myself with confidence.

"Huh? Get the fuck out of here. You're lying."

"No. Remember we were on the same red-eye flight from Los Angeles to Atlanta a few months ago and we were on the tram together afterward? We saw each other but never spoke."

He was convinced it was really me. "Oh, shit! What's up?"

It was just one week after my breakup with Aeron and I was moving on like a champ. Shad and I talked on the phone constantly throughout the day, every day. We text-messaged each other and spent hours each day video chatting, and within a few weeks I was on a first-class flight back to Atlanta to be with him. Everything up until this point had been calculated, but to my surprise, I liked Shad! He was significantly younger than me, and I felt we would have very little in common and very little to talk about, but he was so much more down-to-earth than Wayne. Though he'd been an entertainer most of his life and reached a level of success Wayne may not have as yet, he was real and I instantly adored him.

I arrived in Atlanta the same day I was scheduled to be in court to defend myself against Aeron's felonious restraining-order summons. Legally, I didn't have to appear unless I wanted to fight against the restraining order, and frankly, I was so tired of fighting, and I thought the restraining order was a great idea. With it, Aeron would be ordered to stay away from me just as much as I was being ordered to stay away from him. I was determined to move on with my life. Aeron could say whatever he wanted and file as many orders as he pleased. I was free! As I walked into the baggage claim area of Atlanta's Hartsfield-Jackson International Airport, Shad called me with instructions.

"My people will meet you outside on the curb," he said.

With Wayne, there was always a uniformed chauffeur waiting to greet me at baggage claim and take my luggage before promptly escorting me to a Rolls Royce. This was a definite departure from what I'd become accustomed to, but in a way, I liked it better. I felt like a person visiting another person and not one persona meeting another. I stood on the curb in the hot, muggy Atlanta air for about fifteen minutes before two men in a Chrysler 300 pulled up. I chuckled. It was amateur hour all the way, but I found it endearing.

The driver of the car was Ant, Shad's assistant, who was a bit older than me. In the passenger's seat was a kid who couldn't have been more than nineteen. Neither one of them got out of the car to open the door for me nor offered to grab my luggage.

I just stood there.

And stood there.

"Man, go get her bag!" Ant ordered his young passenger while popping the truck and exiting the car. The other guy mumbled under his breath, totally oblivious as to why it would be customary to carry a woman's luggage *all* the way from the curb to the trunk of the car. Ant came around and opened the back passenger door for me.

Amateur hour, indeed.

On the way to Shad's apartment, Shad called Ant and asked the guys to stop and grab him something to eat. So, there I was, after a long overnight flight, in the back of a Chrysler, in the drive-through line at a fast-food joint. For all Shad's accomplishments and financial gains, he lacked order and refinement; thusly, so did his staff. I could tell, however, that Ant was as annoyed as I was and was apologetic for having to run me around town.

An hour after landing in Atlanta, we pulled up to a high-rise building and made our way through the lobby and into the elevator. As the elevator rose from the ground floor, beeping along the way, I didn't feel nervous. I felt as if I were visiting an old friend. There were no expectations and no need to put on. It was nothing like my first time visiting Wayne. With Wayne, I was terribly nervous and my heart pounded in my chest as I rode the elevator of his high-rise condominium building in Miami. He thrilled me; he excited my senses and made me feel as if I were living in an alternate universe—a universe where there was more pomp and circumstance than reality and normalcy. Everything about Shad was different. So much about his life was normal.

Finally, fast food in one hand and my luggage in another, Ant delivered me to the front door. Shad flung it open and grabbed me, pulling me into him and holding on tightly before taking my bags from Ant and welcoming me into his home for the week. I quickly made myself comfortable, unpacking my things and tidying up the apartment a bit. There must have been a hundred different types of hair on the floor throughout the apartment from all the women who had been there before me.

"Shad!"

"Yes, ma'am?"

"What the hell is all this?" I asked, pointing to the floor.

"What?"

I bent down and pinched a few strands from the floor. "Blonde weaves, brown, and black ones. Curly and straight ones. Indian Remy and Relaxed Texture. I mean, how many different bitches have you fucked in here? And why didn't you have enough sense to Swiffer this shit before I arrived?"

"Had enough sense to do what?"

"Swiffer!"

"Fuck is a Swiffer?" he laughed.

"Do you have a broom?"

"Of course!" Shad walked over to the hall closet and pulled out a broom. "And I have a mop and everything!" he said, proudly.

"And you have a Swiffer!"

He looked in the closet and pulled out the Swiffer. "Oh! That's what this is?"

I shook my head in disbelief and proceeded to show him how to use the Swiffer to clean the floors. Then I inspected the bed. "Shad!"

"Damn. What now?"

"Come in the bedroom."

"What's wrong *now*?" he asked, laughing, as he entered the bedroom.

I pointed to the bed. "There is makeup all over this duvet!"

"What the fuck is a duvet?"

We cracked up at each other. It was a simple moment in time with the kind of conversation had by real people if one of them was nine years younger than the other and extremely sheltered. I proceeded to show Shad the difference between a duvet and a comforter and blew his mind when I explained how a duvet cover can be removed and washed, hence removing the makeup stains of the woman or women who were in his bed before me.

"Do you have a washer and dryer?"

"Yeah. Right over here," he replied proudly as he carried the filthy duvet. Upon opening the washer, we discovered he'd left a load of towels in it for so long, they were mildewed and dry. Shad, young, sheltered, and inexperienced, moved to place the towels in the dryer.

"No! No! No! You can't put those in there!"

"Why not?"

For the next half hour, I taught Shad how to do his laundry. We went through the linen closet removing mildewed towels and rewashing them. The duvet cover was cleaned and placed back on the bed and all was right with the world. My first day with Shad was pretty average. Just two people, being people. We walked around the house in his boxers and T-shirts, acting silly, laughing and joking, playing PlayStation and trolling the Internet for funny blogs and disgusting viral videos like *Two Girls One Cup*.

With Shad, I could be myself. I could say what I wanted, how I wanted, and not worry about sounding foolish or being punished. I felt at home in his home and he never left my side when I was there. Whatever I wanted, whatever I needed, he made sure I had it and he didn't have to hand down orders to his crew to take care of me. We talked about real things. About life and love and all we'd lost along the way. The people who broke our hearts and how much we still hurt, and for the first time, I cried in front of someone.

And he held me.

I cried for all the trauma I'd suffered in every relationship I'd ever had and I cried for the hole in my heart left by the absences of people I'd loved. I cried for Aeron. I cried for Wayne. I cried for myself, for the fortress I had to build and fortify in the wake of the whole world stoning me for decisions I made that weren't so different from their own. I cried and I cried until my stomach hurt.

And he held me.

Then, we made love on the floor, on top of my Gucci luggage.

Shad was inexperienced and shy, young and unlearned in carnal ways, and I liked that. His experience came in the form of caring and catering, in being personable and human. I needed that. Maybe there wasn't as much pomp and circumstance with Shad as there was with Wayne, but there was this—there was simplicity and a sense of normalcy.

I needed that, too.

CHAPTER EIGHT

Lovers and Brothers

For the next three months, Shad and I carried on, keeping our relationship a secret from Wayne, who was all but absent from my life. Every once in a while, I texted Wayne and every once in a while he responded with a word or two. But usually there was nothing. So, I focused on my relationship with Shad, which bordered more on a friendship than anything else. When he was in LA, I often picked him up from his hotel and took him to my house. It would just be us two—no entourage, no pomp. We would wear matching Polo pajama pants and V-neck T's as we lay in bed watching TV or movies, just being. As the relationship became more and more familiar, the romantic side of it subsided but the friendship grew stronger—so strong that I chose to spend my thirtieth birthday in Atlanta that August.

While there, I threw a birthday party at a local club. Shad sent Ant and a few members of his crew to keep an eye on me, making sure I didn't drink too much at my party. For someone so famous, Shad was more of a homebody and opted to stay in his condo, playing video games. Besides, at that time, we were still keeping our friendship a secret from the public. So, he checked in via text message and by making phone calls to see how my party was going and received photos of the event while I celebrated with Ant and his friends.

As always, my trip to Atlanta was a joyous one and it was always fun being around Shad. But, hours before heading to the airport and back to Los Angeles, he gave me the news that would break my heart and tear my soul from my body.

"Your boy Wayne is crazy," he started.

"Why? What did he do now?"

"He got some girl pregnant."

I stopped breathing and tried not to show my pain. "Oh, yeah? Wow."

"Yeah, some chick from Ohio."

"Ohio?"

"Yeah, man. She's about to drop that baby next month!"

Wayne had definitely moved on. I just hadn't guessed to what extent. I tucked this bit of information in the back of my mind and tried not to die from the torment. Wayne and I had been in Ohio about a year before. He had asked me to join him, and true to form, I flew to him with no questions asked. It was our first trip together since Aeron attacked me on my birthday a month or two before. Yet I never saw Wayne during that trip. He kept me in the hotel for three days as he locked himself on his tour bus, presumably with a woman, before leaving town without saying good-bye. I caught the next plane back to Los Angeles, crushed, assuming it was his way of getting back at me for my relationship with Aeron, knowing he had found someone new. When Wayne wanted to hurt me, he knew just how to do it, and as I stood there in Shad's living room nearly a year later, all the pieces were coming together as I was falling apart. I left Atlanta heavyhearted and determined to make Wayne feel what I was feeling. He may have been keeping a secret from me but I had a secret of my own. All I needed was the right set of circumstances and I could break his heart, too.

A month later, Shad visited Los Angeles and I was all too happy to see him again so soon. I dressed and waited for him to call me to let me know when he'd settled into his hotel room. Finally, the phone rang.

"Hello?" I answered

"What's up?" he asked, knowing the answer.

"Waiting on you!"

"Alright. I'm at the Beverly Wilshire, on my bus, but we have a problem."

"What's that?"

"Wayne is here, too."

"Get the fuck out of here."

"Yeah. Our rooms are next door to each other and his bus is parked right in front of mine. I'm looking at it right now. So, try to get to the room without being seen. I'm about to head up there."

"Fuck! Okay." I hung up the phone and felt a chill run down my spine. The hair on my arms stood up and my stomach felt ill.

Truth was, I *wanted* to run into Wayne. In fact, I wanted to *ensure* I would. So, I headed over to the hotel, thinking of what to do. I wanted Wayne to know how badly I was hurt and I wanted him to hurt, too. At the very least, I wanted his ego to feel what my heart felt. I pulled up to the Beverly Wilshire hotel and saw Wayne and Shad's buses parked tandem on the curb. I pulled into the valet, stepped out of the car, and made a beeline for the elevators. Ant was there, waiting to take me to Shad.

In the room, I tried to stay interested as Shad and I watched TV, but all I could think about was Wayne, downstairs on his bus. He was just seconds from me. I hadn't seen him in over six months and I'd needed him so much during that time. I missed him intensely and longed to be even *this* close to him.

But he left me.

He left me.

Shad and I drank beers and got cozy on the couch as we watched TV. Hours passed and Wayne still didn't know I was just seconds away from him. It was eating me up inside that *he* wasn't being eaten up inside. So I sent a text.

I'm in the hotel, I typed.

What hotel?

The Beverly Wilshire, looking down at your bus.

What are you doing here?

I'm in Shad's room. We're about to jump in the shower. Just wanted to say hi. Talk to you later, maybe.

I'd done it.

Now, all I had to do was wait for the fallout. Seconds later, Shad's phone chimed. As he picked it up and looked at it, his mouth flew open.

"Yo, Wayne just texted me and said, *You taking showers with my bitch? I ain't never even took a shower with her!*" Shad put his phone down and walked away, not knowing what to say. After all, what could he say? The wheels were already set in motion and there was nothing we could do to stop them.

Shad and I showered and went to bed. The next morning, I left the hotel and headed home to start my day and get some work done, but I couldn't concentrate. I hadn't heard back from Wayne since I told him I was with Shad. I knew he was upset but I needed to know how upset. I needed to know if he was as upset as I was. I sent a text.

I love you, I wrote.

I love you, too, he responded, surprisingly. *Where are you?*

At home.

Come here, now. I'm on my bus.

Be there in twenty minutes.

I raced to get dressed. I wore a tiny, spaghetti-strapped T and a white, frilly miniskirt. I darted out the door, hopped in my car, and headed back to the Beverly Wilshire. My heart pounded in my chest, wondering what I would say to Wayne, if I would cry, if I would scream, or if I would just fall into his arms, relieved to be with him again. I tried to harden myself in the car, practicing what I would say when I came face-to-face with him.

"I don't love you anymore."

No.

"I didn't miss you at all."

He'd never believe that.

"You left me first!"

Fuck! Truth was, all I wanted to do was hold him and beg him to come back to me. I wanted to tell him that the only reason I was ever with Shad was to make him mad and that all I ever wanted was to be with him. I wanted to ask for forgiveness for things I hadn't even done and take all the responsibility for the way things turned out. I wanted to submit, lie on my back, and take whatever he was willing to give me.

I wanted to, but I couldn't.

Arriving at the hotel, I shuffled toward Wayne's bus. A member of his crew saw me and assumed I was coming to see Wayne, which I was, but not before I stopped in to talk to Shad.

"Hey, Karrine, you coming?" the entourage member said as he held the door to Wayne's bus open for me.

"Yeah, in a second, but I have to see Bow first." He seemed shocked as I knocked on the door of Shad's bus. Once inside, I headed straight to the back where Shad was playing video games with his buddies. "I just wanted to tell you I'm headed over to Wayne's bus."

Shad looked up at me. "Alright, that's cool. Does he know you're going over there?"

"Yeah. He asked me to come see him."

"Okay. Well, I'll be here when you're done."

"Awesome. Be back in a few minutes." I turned and ran out of Shad's bus and toward Wayne's, just a few feet away. I knocked on the door and was let aboard by the same entourage member from earlier, who then exited as I walked in.

"Hey," Wayne said, coming out of the back room to greet me.

"Hey," I returned before falling into his arms. I held onto Wayne and felt his heartbeat against mine, ran my hand across the bullet wound scar on his back, and breathed in the scent of his dreadlocked hair, as I'd done every time I saw him. Everything felt so right, yet so wrong. He was having a baby with another woman and I was seeing his friend. Everything was fucked.

He began to kiss my neck and ran his right hand up my skirt. I shivered and cried, then I backed away from Wayne, tears in my eyes, and said, "I can't do this anymore."

"What do you mean?"

"You left me. Now, I'm leaving you." That said, I walked toward the exit.

"You're not really going to leave, are you?"

I opened the door; the alarm sounded and I ran back to Shad's bus.

That was it.

Wayne and I were over.

CHAPTER NINE

Fear and Loathing

S had and I continued to see each other through the fall and into early 2009. As the months rolled on, the heat in our relationship cooled and he became less available to me, the same as Wayne had before. I would call and text often, with no response, and gone were the times when we'd spend hours video chatting. Shad was slipping away from me as our relationship ran its course, and with Wayne gone, I was getting lonely.

Still, over the past seven months I had been enjoying my freedom and my life without Aeron. It was Shad who got me eating again and it didn't take long for me to regain all the weight I lost while with Aeron. I felt gorgeous and sexy; I felt wanted and cared for when I was with Shad and my confidence was reestablished. I was more aware of my worth and my vitality than I had been in recent years. I felt empowered with Shad just as I had with Wayne. The problem was, I never felt empowered on my own, and with Wayne gone and Shad on his way out, I found myself beginning to feel vulnerable again.

It was early afternoon on January 2, 2009, when I left my perch on the hill and drove to the local donut shop. I was sad that day, not having heard from Shad in almost a week and regretting letting Wayne walk out of my life. I needed comfort food. So I pulled up to the donut shop, located in a shopping center just minutes from my home, and hopped out of my Range Rover in a white sweat suit. My body stretched my sweat pants to their limit as I shuffled into the shop, unaware I was being watched. Moments later, with a dozen donuts in hand, I hopped into my SUV and made my way back home, content to spend the rest of the day in bed with my newly acquired confections. I undressed and wrapped my hair in a silk scarf, prepared to shove several donuts and bear claws down my throat and just lie there. But seconds after climbing under the covers with my pink box of sugary snacks, there was a heavy knock at the door.

I jumped, then paused. I was almost certain I'd closed the gate behind me after pulling into the garage and checked the alarm system to make sure it was engaged. My heart pounded as I slid out of bed and crept toward the front door, trying to avoid creaking floorboards. I poked my head around the corner, looking at the front door, which was made of heavily smoked glass. I could see an imposing figure standing there, tall and broad. Whoever he was, he would have had to jump my six-foot, spiked gate, if closed, to get to my front door. The thought bothered me but I had a sneaking suspicion who he might be and called out to the alarming figure in my most menacing voice: "Who is it?"

"It's Aeron."

"Who?" I asked, unsure my hearing was correct.

"Aeron."

"Who?" I asked, again, in a state of disbelief.

"Aeron! Aeron!"

"Hold on," I commanded as I ripped the scarf from my head, brushed my hair, and slipped on my white sweatpants. "Coming!" I announced as I gathered my senses, my heart pounding in my chest, my pet pit bull, Jolie, scurrying to the front door. I took a deep breath, held Jolie by her collar, and opened the door to find Aeron standing there, seven months after he ran over my foot with his car, seven months after he took out a restraining order against me.

"Hey," he said.

"Hey."

"How are you?"

"Perfect and gorgeous."

"Yes, you are."

"What are you doing here?" I asked as I looked beyond the entrance way to the gate, seeing it closed and his car parked along the curb. "And how did you get in here? You jumped the gate?"

"I did. I came to check on you."

"I'm fine. I don't need to be checked up on."

"Can I come in?" he asked as I held Jolie back from attacking him with wet doggy kisses.

"Sure."

As he walked into my home, he began to explain himself. "I was at the Verizon store, getting a new phone, and I saw this woman hop out of a white Range Rover in these white sweatpants with a fat butt and I couldn't keep my eyes off her. She went into the donut shop and I watched as she ordered her donuts and walked out."

"Oh, really?" I asked, with a smirk on my face.

"Yeah. I was thinking about running out to the parking lot and talking to her until I realized it was you. You gained your weight back. It looks good!"

"I know. Go on."

"So, when I realized it was you, I hesitated for a little bit. I got my new phone and watched you drive away. I was going to just go about my business but I couldn't let you get away from me. So I decided to follow you home and here I am!"

It was amazing. It never fails, really. Every time you get past an ex, they miraculously pop back into your life at the precise moment you don't think you need them anymore. It's as if they have some sort of radar. Aeron was always good at this, at feeling out the exact moment when I might be on the mend and coming back into my life to finish me off. It was as if he was thinking, *How dare she be okay without me. How dare she gain all her weight back and then some and be happy with some other man or men or even by herself. How dare she move on and get over me after all I've put her through.* He hated to see me well, and our relationship, from the very start, was a game of seek and destroy—a sick version of Battleship in which I was the only blip on the sonar and I was the only one who stood to lose everything.

Everything.

But I was lonely.

Wayne was gone and Shad was obviously no longer interested and I just didn't want to be alone. So, I let Aeron back into my home and into my life. He said all the right things, everything I needed to hear. He made apologies and promises and admitted to his wrong-doings. He told me about a church he wanted us to join and how much Jonah missed Naiim and me. He talked about getting married, having children of our own, standing up to his mother, and keeping our family together. Aeron tugged on every fucking heartstring I had and I buckled under the weight of my hope.

A month later, I called Shad to tell him our relationship was over. "I'm getting back with my ex," I said, softly.

"What? Get the fuck out of here! After all the shit he put you through? I sat here and watched you cry about all the shit he did to you and you're going to go back to that motherfucker?"

"Well, you and I haven't been talking much. You don't even check for me like you used to, so I'm going back to where I belong."

"Man, you don't belong with that man! I was just saying to myself I should call you and fly you out here to chill. I mean, I know we haven't been talking as much. I've been an asshole and I know it. But come on, K!"

Shad warned me emphatically and tried to convince me to change my mind and hop on the next flight to Atlanta, if for no other reason than to save me from myself and from the man who'd done nothing but torture and abuse me. But I'd already let Aeron back in and, as he stood there listening to Shad scream at me through the speakerphone, he smirked, knowing he had me back in his grips. All it had taken was talk of being better than before and cleverly placed promises to make our family official by getting married, exactly what I'd wanted to hear my entire adult life.

From then forward, I became obsessed with the thought of it all. Aeron knew my voids and continued to dangle emotional carrots, and I continued to chase them around and around, again and again. We spent the first thirty days after he returned holed up at home, making up for lost time. I looked past all the things that happened before and focused on the future. I wanted to believe him, so I did, and to me, there would be only one way to prove that this time around was for real. There would be only one way to show the world that, after all the shit he talked about me, after all the abuse I took from him, he did, in fact, love me and that I wasn't wrong for loving him. I wanted to prove I was lovable and worthy of the family I never had. I wanted the world to see me as I saw myself, the same as any woman.

So, for the next three months, I never let a day go by without reminding Aeron about his promise to marry me. I called chapels and gathered information and came up with the easiest way to make it all happen. I found out that, in the city of Los Angeles, one could just walk into a local chapel and get married, the same as in Las Vegas, and for just over three hundred dollars. Aeron and I already had rings, the matching diamond and sapphire ones I'd purchased the year before, and I chose a chapel just twenty minutes away. I bugged Aeron. I pressured him. I begged him, until finally, on March 23, 2009, he gave in and we were wed in a private, walk-in ceremony.

We wore jeans and T-shirts.

Jonah, just less than two years old, was with us. My son spent his day in school, unaware. It was all very last minute and I hurried to get us to the chapel before Aeron changed his mind. He drove. I suppose I knew he didn't really want to marry me and I knew I shouldn't be marrying him, much less dating or living with him, but I just needed it all to look perfect. Even if it was shit on the inside, the outside needed to seem ideal. We didn't tell anyone, no friends or family, knowing they would only disapprove, all for different reasons, none of them wrong.

As the officiant pronounced us husband and wife, I grabbed Aeron's face with both hands as he held Jonah, and kissed his lips through grateful tears. "Thank you," I said, softly.

His face was cold as he disconnected.

The resentment was instant.

CHAPTER TEN

Things We Lost

"Are you happy?" I asked, grabbing Aeron's hand as it gripped the gearshift of my SUV. He was driving us back home and, as Jonah watched a movie in the backseat, Aeron stared at the road silently. "Are you happy?" I asked, again.

"You know what? I am. I'm very happy," he said, the same cold, disconnected look upon his face.

I continued holding Aeron's hand all the way home, trying to lighten the mood, but he seemed to be sinking further into an abyss of contempt. By the time we pulled into my garage, he was angry. Fuming. Soon after returning home, we began arguing.

"Well, I hope you're happy now," he scoffed as he laid next to me in bed, changing channels on the television with the remote. "You got what you wanted; this is what you wanted. Now you're going to have a sexless marriage like everyone else who's married, because I'm never touching you again."

I sobbed, "Why are you acting like this? You said you wanted to get married. Sure, I didn't want to wait but *you're* the one who drove us down there! You're acting like I forced you!"

"You did! And I hope you're proud of yourself. I hope you enjoy having a marriage like my mother and my father had, a miserable one, because that's what marriage is—two miserable fucking people joined together by a piece of paper. It doesn't mean anything!"

I continued to sob as my husband berated me, hopping out of bed and walking around to my side. Sitting there, my knees to my chest, my head buried in them, I cried, begging Aeron to stop, to lie back down and relax. But he continued to rant, to make clear his disdain for me, the sanctity of marriage, and our nuptials. I was his third wife, and he promised me, on our wedding day, I would be his third divorce.

Then, with hate in his eyes, my husband spit on me.

He spit in my face and so I spit back. With Jonah in the other room, he lunged for me, for my throat, and began to apply pressure with his forearm, the weight of his 215-pound frame applied to my neck. He was crazed as I gasped for air, as I kicked and clawed at his arm, digging my nails into his face, trying to get him off me, trying to survive another attack. I coughed and struggled, growing dizzy and close to unconsciousness. Then Aeron released me. Afraid for my life, I ran out of the bedroom, grabbed the car keys from the entranceway table, and fled into the garage. I locked myself inside my Mercedes sedan and called our church's pastor for help.

This was my wedding day.

Aeron hadn't kept most of his promises, but we did join a local church and found ourselves there most every Sunday for a while. We must have looked like a real family, walking in with our two children, praising and worshiping together. It must have looked so normal. But Aeron hated the church and not just that church. He harbored a disdain for churches in general. He spoke of how his father was the musical director for one of the largest black churches in Los Angeles and how Aeron gave so much of his money and time to that church. He spoke about the things he'd seen so-called saved souls do after church hours and all the hypocrisy that existed in organized religion. Aeron held so much disdain for so many things that he tended to make everything displeasing. He spoke often of the way his father cheated on his mother with women close to the family and many other random women and how, every Sunday, his shattered family was all expected to show up at church and act as if nothing was wrong. Aeron had been acting all his life, on and off the stage, and now I was acting, too.

Our pastor came to the house on our wedding day to counsel us as he had done before we were married. Usually, during these sessions, the things Aeron said and the way he saw the world were so terribly skewed that no one could have agreed with his logic. The pastor would side with me and this would only infuriate Aeron. This time, our pastor managed to calm the situation, but the damage had already been done. In fact, the damage had been done two years before. I'd made a horrible mistake going back to Aeron and I knew it, but I just couldn't quit—I couldn't give up on the idea of being fucking normal. So I stayed with Aeron and the cycle continued. Soon, there was no one I could talk to about our relationship—not even the pastor. It made no sense to complain about something so horrible only to stay. So, in June 2009, I began to keep a journal of the abuse, instead.

June 25, 2009: Aeron's financial contributions to our marriage have been sporadic, and when he does contribute, more often than not, it falls short of the mark. Aeron has not been living in the home for over a month. He came to visit me today at 2 PM and left at 2:50 PM. To date, he has threatened to take half my money, should we divorce this month. Just ninety days into the marriage, I suspect money is the reason he married me in the first place. Last week, he threatened to file for divorce. I told him to do so if he pleased—he has not. Now he acts as if the conversation never took place. Aeron often takes the baby from his bed in the middle of the night and at dawn (9 PM, 1 AM, 4 AM) to travel with him to music studios.

June 26, 2009 (12:15 AM): Aeron has promised to be home tonight and has not shown, nor is he reachable by phone anymore. When questioned about his timeframe for coming home he replied, "MJ (Michael Jackson) is dead, bitch!" This response has prompted me to ask that he not return home until he is prepared to live a righteous life and be a husband according to God's word and rejoin our church, which he has neglected for two months.

July 2, 2009 (4:57 PM): Aeron finally showed up this past Sunday, two hours late, for church. He stayed until Monday afternoon. He was ill during that time with chest pains, heart murmurs, and extreme exhaustion. I nursed him both days. Today is Thursday and he has not returned. He calls maybe once a day but only after I have called him or texted repeatedly. He says he is now in Malibu, has had his car towed to the shop, and is depressed. He says he sleeps all day and night. As of 5:02 PM, I have not heard from my husband at all today. I have called four times and sent one text message. I am not sure if he will be here for the Fourth of July as he has promised. I feel completely abandoned and alone, uncared for and unappreciated. Neither our marriage nor I exist to him.

July 11, 2009: Aeron and I spent the Fourth of July with the kids and his family. It was awesome. I was happy to be included. The kids had so much fun. Later that night, he and Jonah came home and stayed the night. They stayed the next day, as well, and Aeron even left Jonah with Naiim and me for a portion of the day while he took meetings. Over the past week, he has shown massive improvements.

Six months and many, many physical altercations later, I prepared to move out of my home. It was August 2009 and the real estate bubble had burst. I bought my home in 2006 and maintained over $20,000 in bills and mortgage payments over the past three years with no help from Aeron during the times he lived with me, nor after we were married. He continued to live for free and use me and I continued to let him.

At the same time, one of my mortgage payments, which I assumed had been paid, wasn't. That made it impossible for me to refinance my home when my ARM fluctuated, and my mortgage payments increased. When my mortgage company was bought out during the real estate crash, it made it impossible for me to modify my payment, an option set aside for those with trouble paying their bills. My mortgage jumped from $6,000 a month to $10,000 and it was just too much for me to bear alone.

My entire life seemed to be in the hands of other people and it was quickly being derailed. Aeron was rarely even home as I struggled to pay the current mortgage and find a new home before putting my house up for sale—all the while taking care of him and his son, as he continued to be primarily unemployed.

I refrained from paying the mortgage in May and prepared to move into a newer, larger, less expensive home with the money I saved by not paying the bills at my current home. When the time came to pack up and move, Aeron was nowhere to be found. He was there with me when I found the home and toured it with me the day I handed over the check to the owners of the rental property. He contributed $1,500 to the $15,000 move-in cost. It wasn't much, but it seemed he was trying. Soon, though, he became frustrated with his financial shortcomings and his inability to help me do much of anything during this stressful time, so he picked a fight with me and left just before moving day.

It was all very typical.

So I handled the move all alone. The new home was significantly larger, boasting three stories and over 6,000 square feet. The home was built into a hillside so each story was built down instead of up, with the main entrance, common areas, and guest room on the top floor, the master and two other bedrooms downstairs on the second floor, and a complete studio apartment down on the third floor. It was the perfect size for Aeron, the kids, and me, with an entire third-floor apartment that could serve as an office for me, and a recording studio for Aeron. I was trying so hard to make it all work and to give Aeron reasons to come home and stay home more often. I bought more furniture to fill my new temple, my homage to a life I didn't really have. I put the new clothes in the closets. I set up a new room for Jonah with a brand-new bed and dresser, toy box and toys. It was all so perfect; every room looked like the cover of a magazine.

But four of the six bedrooms remained empty.

CHAPTER ELEVEN

Soap Operas and Porn

*A*bout a month and a half after Naiim and I moved into the new home, Aeron and Jonah moved in, too, though their version of moving in was more of an extended sleepover. Aeron soon developed a pattern of staying at home for a few weeks, then disappearing for two. I'd become so accustomed to the dysfunction and his misuse of me that I began looking forward to his return, being grateful even, after reeling over each disappearance. His reasons for returning were always the same. He would spend weeks traveling and bouncing from one place to the next. He would live with his mother for weeks at a time until, eventually, she drove him away with her controlling influence. He would spend time with his sister, Samantha, and her husband and son as well as his brother, Jonathan, his girlfriend and their children. Naturally, there were long nights in recording studios and, I suspect, lots of other women. It was only when he got tired of living this way that he would come home to rest. With me, there was quiet and order; the kids were taken care of, food was cooked, laundry was done, everything was paid for, and the house ran on a very productive schedule. He craved that at the end of his trysts and vagabond adventures.

I was nothing more than my husband's rest stop.

Soon after his return, I helped Aeron prepare for an audition for a long-running soap opera on the CBS television network, which I'd been watching since I was six years old. I knew all about the character for whom he was auditioning and reprising. I worked with him for hours over a few days and gave him much-needed background information on the character and his relationship with the other characters in the soap. Aeron was well prepared when he left home for the audition and I prayed he would get the job. I needed him to have steady work and I know he needed it, too. I thought that maybe he would feel better about himself if he was able to contribute in a significant way to the household. I thought that if he landed the series, he'd keep a better schedule and would be more apt to come home every day and participate in the home and the hope I'd been building for us.

I was still hoping he would change.

Still.

Days after his audition, Aeron announced he'd be leaving town for a couple weeks. He never explained all the reasons why he was leaving or to where he'd be traveling, but I knew he planned on visiting his grandmother in Texas before returning to Los Angeles. He left town with the new manager he'd recently hired, a man with a sketchy background who promised him ridiculous things like a spot as the opening act for Michael Jackson's *This Is It* tour, before the pop icon died. Aeron believed everything this man said, no matter how ridiculous and unfounded. This new manager told Aeron he'd be going on tour with all sorts of acts, like TLC, and he just figured it all must have been true. That's how diluted and distorted Aeron's view of the world and grip on reality was—that's how badly he wanted to be a musical act instead of an actor. This manager also told Aeron he'd be able to help him erect his own musical, which is what the two of them were doing during that trip—searching for venues, stage props, and whatnot. It was all so very confusing as I watched Aeron chase dreams and follow the guidance of strange men—men he would always call Pops or Uncle—as he always reeled from the father who had left him over twenty years before. Aeron was a confused and broken man with demons and secrets swirling about his head, and for the sake of family and the appearance of normalcy, I continued to force a relationship with him.

Two weeks turned into three and three weeks turned into six as I fought to stay in contact with my husband. He rarely answered the phone and never returned phone calls and text messages. I felt tortured as I waited to hear from him, pacing around my big, empty house. I'd fallen back into my normal self-destructive routine since Aeron came back into my life earlier that year. It was difficult for me to eat in times of stress and I lost all the weight I gained when I was with Shad, hovering around only 100 pounds. My hair became thin and my nails brittle and I drank red wine by the case. I resumed smoking cigarettes. I was back to taking Xanax to help me sleep and stay calm as I nervously waited to hear from my husband. All this distress showed clearly on my face and in my eyes.

Then, after not hearing from Aeron for weeks, he called.

"Hello?" I answered.

"Aye," he said, in his deep, burly voice. "Listen, I want a divorce. This just isn't working for me. I mean, I didn't want to get married in the first place."

My heart sank as I listened to my husband say the same things he'd been saying since the day we got married. Part of me knew it was inevitable and a part of me wanted it to never happen. If he wanted to file for divorce, there was nothing I could do. In Los Angeles County, there is no stopping a divorce, unless the person filing changes his or her mind. And since Aeron and I shared nothing, there would be nothing to fight over. He could file, and within six months our divorce would be final, no matter how I felt about it. After all he'd done and all I'd gone through, I should have been pleased to hear I was about to get another chance to save my life, but instead, I felt more broken than ever before. All I could say was, "Okay." I hung up the phone that day, not knowing when or if Aeron would return.

I grieved for the next week, lying in bed with the curtains drawn, wishing I could go back to the summer of 2007, to Aeron and my first kiss. I wished I could undo it all. I wanted so badly to crawl out of my skin. It hurt to be me. I cried every day, all throughout the day, and drank myself to sleep every night. So many times over the past two years with Aeron, I'd thought about suicide and how easy it would be to deliver myself from the pain I was in. Then I would think about my son finding me and how the rest of his life would be ruined. I figured at least one of us deserved a chance to be happy and I wanted to give that chance to him.

But I couldn't do it in this condition.

In November, about a week after Aeron announced he wanted a divorce, I opened up my laptop and clicked onto my personal Facebook page to find an article written by my old friend Jawn Murray reporting that Aeron had gotten the job as a series regular on the soap opera for which I helped him prepare. It was my first time hearing the news and my mouth flew open as I connected the dots. My husband was going to divorce me now that he had a job, a two-year contract with CBS. After everything I did, after all the money I spent on him and Jonah, he was leaving me now that it seemed he would be able to pay his own bills.

It made perfect sense.

Why didn't you tell me you got the job? I wrote in a text to Aeron.

Because I couldn't tell anyone, he responded. *How did you find out?*

The Internet. So, now that you have a job, you want a divorce?

No. I've always wanted a divorce.

But you couldn't file because you needed me to pay your bills and buy your clothes and take care of your son . . .

Fuck you, Karrine. See you in court.

But that's not exactly what happened. When Aeron returned to Los Angeles, in the midst of the negotiation of his contract with the network, it turned out he wouldn't be making nearly as much as he expected during his first year on the show, and after agency and management fees, he would still be scraping the bottom. So, in late November, he came back home and I took care of him.

The consistent money he was now making was more than he'd made during the entire course of our relationship. Aeron had worked sporadically while we were living together and as soon as he got a check, it would be gone. He would give money to his mother, who was still a signee on his bank accounts as she had been since he was a child. He would take care of himself, his immediate family, and Jonah, but never me. The same applied when he began filming the soap in November. He filmed several times a week and was paid bi-weekly. Yet I never saw a dime and I rarely saw him.

As the holiday season came and went, my husband was absent, as usual. Naiim and I spent Thanksgiving alone only to have Aeron come over two days later with a plate of leftover food from his mother's house. Leftovers. Mona owned him and he would always be more her husband than he ever would be mine. He knew that I didn't have any family, that I'd alienated all my friends because of our abusive relationship, and that I'd be spending the holidays alone. He knew he was all I had and he used that fact to continuously break me down and remind me how alone I was. Naturally, Aeron was also absent that Christmas and New Year. Still, I stayed put, in that shrine of a home, worshiping a marriage that didn't exist, waiting for my husband to return.

And he always did.

November 24, 2009: I have not seen my husband for one month and one day. He does not call regularly. He does not check on Naiim, ever. He is abusive, verbally and emotionally. He hangs up on me with no provocation. He says he wants a divorce but wants to still be together and not tell anyone we're divorced. Aeron was doing so well for a while. He left on August 20, 2009, until the end of September. He went to San Diego and Mexico for two days with no phone calls. I don't know where he lives. I don't know anything about him. I keep asking him to come home but he won't. He refuses. I have lost ten pounds. I am so stressed.

November 30, 2009 (10:20 AM): Aeron came home around 1:45 AM, November 29th and brought Jonah with him. It was my first time seeing them in five weeks. Aeron was in good spirits and I was happy to see both my boys. We talked and made love for the first time in five weeks. The next morning, we ate, fed the baby, and made love once more. We talked about our jobs and Jonah's custody situation. We remained in good spirits. The baby was clinging to me. He seemed to really miss Naiim and me and asked to stay with me. He cried when they left.

December 7, 2009: Aeron and I spent most of the day with the kids. It was nice. He seemed very distracted and flustered with stuff in his life. He took Jonah and said he'd be back but never came. He stood me up.

December 11, 2009: Aeron went to a red carpet, again, without me and without wearing his wedding ring. It is so embarrassing when journalists and friends call, asking why he never takes me anywhere, as if he's ashamed. This is the fourth time he has done this and it hurts. When I bring it to his attention, he says he doesn't care or understand what I'm talking about. He said, "I have nothing to say about it," and hung up. The emotional disregard is unbearable.

December 14, 2009: Aeron promised to come by last night but never made it. Again, he says he wants a divorce, but doesn't want to leave me. Yet he has not moved back home. Naiim is becoming affected by his absence and Aeron's attachment to Jonah only. We have not had sex in weeks—just once in eight weeks. I asked him to not keep the relationship or me in limbo, to either "reel me in or cut me loose," because this is too painful. He says he wants to be with me, he just doesn't know how. I said that actually being with me might be a good start. I gave him twenty-four hours to make his decision. He says he "doesn't want to be married on paper." He says I forced this marriage on him, yet he is the one who drove us to the chapel that morning. I don't understand. I have been patient and I have allowed him to come and go as he pleases, but the non-commitment is becoming a strain. He has left me more than he has stayed. No help for food or bills at all, before or after the marriage. No regard for what marriage means. I married him for better or worse—for a lifetime. My life, my marriage, is not a game or a joke to me. I don't know if I can go on. He says his work is more important and I'm not sure I can compete.

December 18, 2009: Aeron came by on the thirteenth and helped me season meat for dinner. He also took a few of his belongings he left behind two weeks prior when he spent the night. He came by on the fourteenth and went with me to the hardware store for ant killer and helped me lay it around the house, before borrowing my Range Rover. He's had it ever since and has parked his car in the garage. It has some mechanical issues. I have asked him to stop by, tonight, for a date night. I am trying to reconnect with my husband and save our marriage by showing him it is not the document that ruined our relationship—it was us and all the pressures of our lives that have changed us. I'm hoping this night will propel us to fall in love again.

December 31, 2009: Aeron promised to come home for Christmas Eve. He didn't, nor did he come home for Christmas, as promised. Now it's New Year's Eve. He promised he'd come. I guess I'll know soon enough.

January 1, 2010: Aeron never showed up last night. I brought the New Year in alone and in tears. He said he was at the emergency room with exhaustion and dehydration. He didn't even want me by his side. I don't even know where he lives! This is no marriage, and now I am begging him to stop threatening to file for divorce and just do it. It is obvious he doesn't care about me no matter what I've done to accommodate him. I have given him all the space and time he demanded and he can't even spend holidays with me, nor does he lean on me during emergencies. We are not a team. This marriage is a joke and all I want is to save it. But I can't do it alone. I am broken.

January 10, 2010: Aeron came by at 3:30 AM on the sixth. He came through the backyard and tapped on the bedroom's back door. He scared me. He said he was coming to drop off two shirts he bought Naiim for Christmas. Both shirts were way too small. He doesn't even know his own step-son's size! He asked to stay and I let him. He asked to have sex with me and I refused. He only uses me for sex. He misses holidays and birthdays but shows up when he's horny. This is so unfair! I was not very warm toward him, given his treatment of this marriage and me. He has not spoken to me since. He ignores all my calls and text messages. I just want him to be a good friend, husband, and dad. He is neither and I am still broken. Lonely. Needing love.

January 16, 2010: Aeron came by on the evening of the thirteenth. He said he would no longer be using a cellphone. I know he was lying, since he would need to contact Jonah in case of emergencies. I have no way of contacting him except for emails, which he never answers. He helped me jump my car while he was here and went with me to fill up the tank before he took off. It was an hour-long visit, at best. It's now been three days and I haven't heard from him. Naiim's twelfth birthday is in three days. I'm wondering if Aeron will remember or show up.

In mid-January of 2010, Aeron came back to the house to celebrate Naiim's twelfth birthday with us. Where he'd been and what he'd done while he was gone was, as always, a mystery. I never asked. There was so much I never knew about my husband—his whereabouts, his cohorts. He lied about everything, all the time, and I believed everything he said, every time he said it.

And there were women.

Lots of them.

So, on February 1, 2010, when Aeron left his email account open after using my computer, I couldn't resist. Though he'd spend as much as seven months away from home at a time and I'd come across inappropriate text messages between him and other women, he always insisted he was faithful. I suppose I always knew he was lying but I still felt the need for more proof, so I went looking for it.

It didn't take long for me to find more than what I was looking for, as I came across many inappropriate messages from a bevy of women and a particularly disturbing stream of emails between my husband and a nearly 300-pound pornographic performer who works under the name Felicia Fats. I felt physically sick as I began reading the emails between them and opening the bevy of lewd, pornographic photos and videos Felicia Fats had sent to my husband.

I fell onto the floor as I read, disgusted by my husband's conduct and his flagrant disregard for our marriage and our children. My body began to shake and tears fell from my eyes as I fought back the urge to vomit.

Their conversation, mixed with the graphic visuals, proved too much for my stomach. I couldn't go on; I'd seen enough. I ran to the bathroom, slumped over the toilet, and threw up. I hugged the cold, white porcelain bowl as I sat, my legs shaking, banging against the travertine floors. Hot and acidic, the vomit tore through my throat like lava, consisting of nothing more than bile. I hadn't eaten in days, nearly a week. It had been a task to ingest even water.

I'd done everything I could to be a good wife and mother. I'd supported my husband in every way I knew how. I cooked, I cleaned, I paid *all* the bills and made sure he and the kids had everything they needed. I was always available to him, always home, always ready to receive him whenever he decided to come back to me. I changed everything I was for him and endured years of shaming and belittling by him and his family, to say nothing of the physical abuse— the beatings, the choking, the spitting. Now, there I was in this shrine I called our home, these three stories and 6,000 square feet of emptiness dedicated to the idea of the perfect family. There I was in the prison I built for myself *on* purpose, *for* the purpose of being finally loved and finally fucking normal.

There I was, being anything but.

CHAPTER TWELVE

What Has Changed

My heart raced as I crawled back to the living room and to the phone to call my spiritual life coach and closest confidant, Deneen. She and I met through mutual friends back in 2001 while she was vacationing in Los Angeles from Birmingham, Alabama. From the moment we became acquainted, we were drawn to one another. She was almost old enough to be my mother and possessed very mothering qualities, though she had no children of her own. So, I became her daughter. Deneen was very spiritually grounded, and no matter what my issue or circumstance, she always treated me with love and respect and was always teaching me about God.

I was wild back then and it took me over a decade to begin to fully understand everything Deneen had been teaching me, but she never gave up. She was always there for my good days as well as my bad, and there was no one else I could call to help me through what was happening now. I dialed her number hastily and paced as I waited for her to answer the phone, tears streaming down my face.

Finally, she answered. "Hello, baby!"

She could barely understand a word I said as I rattled off the details of what I found in Aeron's email. I told her about the disgusting pictures and videos and the upsetting set of emails between my husband and the obese porn star. I spoke quickly, choking on my words and drowning in my tears.

"Calm down," she started. "Take a breath and listen to me. Now, let me ask you this. What has changed?"

My sobs subsided and, for a few seconds, I couldn't breathe as I was overwhelmed by the question. "What do you mean?" I asked.

"Look around and tell me what has changed since you read those emails. Have you lost anything? Or are you still in your home with your son and still in possession of all your achievements and all your graces? Look around. What have you lost?"

"Nothing," I whispered through my sniffles.

"Right. And have you received any new information today?"

"Yeah, I did!"

"Did you? Did you really find out something about Aeron you didn't already know?"

I thought about that, and as simple as the question was, it was all so profound. "No, I knew all of this already. I mean, maybe I didn't know about this particular thing, but this is Aeron, always has been."

"Okay," Deneen said with a sense of relief in her voice. "Nothing has changed and there is no new information here, so why are you so worked up? Stay calm, call him, tell him to come home, and have a conversation with him about this, rationally."

It took everything inside me to do as instructed. My blood coursed and my body ran hot for the two hours it took for Aeron to return home after I insisted there was an emergency with my son, knowing the truth would only prevent him from coming. I stood by the bay window overlooking the driveway as his blue, late-model Jaguar pulled up to the curb. Still on the phone with Deneen, I rushed her off and assumed the proper positioning in my mind—calm and collected. I placed myself on the sofa, my laptop open to the emails, and waited for him to come through the door. I said a silent prayer, asking God for strength and patience.

As he walked in, I sat there, somber.

"What's going on?" he asked. "Is the boy okay?"

"He's fine. Sit down. I have to talk to you about something."

As he sat, I began to read from the string of emails between him and Felicia Fats. Tears streamed down my face and I heaved with the need to vomit again, still disgusted by the images of anal sex and self-fisting the super-fat porn performer had sent him. I waited for my husband to shrink; I waited for him to be embarrassed after being found out, but no.

Instead, he laughed at me.

"You think this is funny?" I questioned, as I grew angrier, trying to restrain myself when all I wanted to do was beat him to death with my Macintosh. Yet, I knew that if I showed any sign of anger, it would anger him, too, and he'd hit me for sure. I remained calm and kept my voice quiet, not wanting to rile the giant.

"Yeah, it's funny!" he replied snidely with a huge grin, proud of himself and the hurt he'd inflicted.

"So, you don't think this is an inappropriate conversation for a married man to have with another woman, much less a three-hundred-pound sex-worker?"

"Nah. I don't see anything inappropriate about it. It was just a joke. It's nothing."

"A joke? Nothing? You think talking to a woman about all the sex you want to have with her is a joke? You think hurting me is nothing?"

"Yep."

My husband laughed—I mean, *really* laughed—as I sat there and wept, withering under the weight of yet another personal and marital defeat. All I could do was cry and keep crying. We sat there, talking and debating until the sun went down and into the wee hours of the morning. I fumed and Aeron wallowed in my pain like a pig in slop. I went over all the horrible and hurtful things he did and said in the three years we'd been together that had torn me apart, diminished my esteem, and doomed our marriage and the future of our family. I pleaded for him to hear me, to please be the husband I deserved, to treat me better, to come home at night, and to help put our family back together.

He laughed.

Eventually, we both tired and walked down to the second story of the house, into the master suite, and crawled into bed. Somewhere along the way, I'm sure he promised to be a better man and husband. I'm sure he swore to never be unfaithful. I'm sure he said all the things that he thought I needed to hear so I'd just shut the fuck up and go to sleep. But as I lay there, next to this man whom I both loved and hated, it all came rushing back to me and the tears returned.

With my fists, I pounded on his thighs, screaming, "Why do you do this to me? Why?"

Aeron sprang up from his resting position and pushed me off the bed and onto the floor. He darted to his jeans, which were flung over the bed's footboard, and drew his belt from its loops. As I lay on the floor, crying, my husband stood over me and began beating me with his belt. I screamed and held my hands outward, trying to grasp the belt to no avail.

"You want to act like a child," he said, "then I'm going to treat you like one," as he continued whipping me.

"Aeron! Stop! Please! You're hurting me! Stop!" I yelled out as he relentlessly continued striking me. The thick leather curled around my arms, back, and neck as it struck me, leaving burning, stinging welts on my skin.

"Is this what you want?" he asked as he kept lashing. "You like this, huh?" he taunted as the blows became more powerful. Aeron continued beating me until we were interrupted by my son, who had awoken from his sleep and crept out of his bedroom in the midst of all the commotion and upon hearing his mother's cries.

Just twelve years old, Naiim barged through the bedroom door, afraid but brave. "Is everything alright in here?" he asked, already knowing the answer.

As I lay on the floor in a fetal position, my husband standing over me, belt in hand, I assured my son I was alright, even though both he and I knew it was a lie. "Mommy's okay, baby. Go back to bed."

As my son closed the door, being too young and too small to fight his six-foot-four stepfather, Aeron grabbed my left arm and brought me to my feet.

"Now, take your ass to bed," he snarled.

I crawled into bed, sobbing and shaking, and curled into a familiar fetal position, my back turned to my husband. He flopped into bed and lay on his back for a few moments before rolling over and scooting his large frame directly behind me. I lay on my side as he pressed himself against my body, his rock-hard manhood pressing against my backside. He was turned on by the beating he'd administered and there was nothing I could do against his advances; with Aeron, I was powerless, and no matter what he did, he was always allowed to use me, body and soul.

He removed my panties, sliding them gently past my thighs and down to my ankles before parting my legs and easing inside me. With my back turned to him, my husband had sex with me just as we had countless nights before—like a scratched and warped record—two bodies so wrong for one another but too familiar to disengage. I cried as my husband took even more from me, never satisfied, never having taken enough.

When we awoke later that morning, we both acted as if nothing happened. I wanted it to be over. I wanted to believe his apologies and promises. I wanted to be happy with my husband and for him to be happy with me. Exhausted from our sixteen-hour conversation and physical ordeal, I lay in bed as Aeron scurried around the house getting ready for work. As I dozed in and out of sleep, I could hear him coming in and out of the house, going to and from his car. Looking at the clock, I realized it was time to cart my son off to school, so I shuffled out of bed, dressed, and walked into Naiim's room. I couldn't bear to look at him. I knew he'd seen too much. He'd heard and seen so much abuse between Aeron and me, and I knew I owed him better but was too weak to give it to him.

"Come on, babe. Time to go," I said as I ushered him out of his bedroom and up the stairs to the first floor where Aeron was waiting for us.

"Alright, then. I'll call you later," Aeron assured as he kissed my forehead. "Have a good day in school, man," he said as he rubbed my son on the top of his head. Damaged, Naiim just nodded.

The three of us got into two separate cars and drove off in two separate directions. Our home was in the center of a hillside road shaped like a horseshoe, and as I reached the bottom of the hill on the left side, I looked to the right. Aeron's car should have arrived at the bottom of the hill, as well, and when I didn't see him, I waited for a few moments. When his car still didn't appear, I got the instinct to turn around and head back to the house. Something told me he'd returned, but I didn't listen to that sixth sense and instead went on my way.

The ride to my son's school was quiet for the most part with the exception of me making excuses for Aeron once again. "Last night scared you, huh?" I asked my twelve-year-old.

"Yeah."

"I know. I'm sorry, babe. We were arguing but it wasn't serious. Okay?"

"Okay," he said, just trying to appease me.

"That won't happen again, though. I promise."

"Okay."

He didn't believe me, and neither did I.

I dropped my son off at school and rushed back to the house. I still had the feeling that something wasn't right and that Aeron may have gone back after I'd pulled off. I sped into the driveway, swung into the garage, and raced into the house. I began looking for signs that he'd returned; I thought maybe he would have packed up his and Jonah's belongings to take back to Mona's house, where Jonah was staying. I ran down the stairs and into the master bedroom. He hadn't taken anything. Checking Jonah's closet, nothing had been taken from there either. It seemed I was just paranoid. Maybe Aeron had made it off the hill before I did and hadn't turned back, after all.

Our relationship was driving me crazy.

I went upstairs to the living room to retrieve my laptop and do my best to carry on with my day. I was in the midst of writing a pilot script for Fox Television Studios based on my third book, *The Vixen Manual*. After the studio optioned the title and signed me to a development deal back in 2008, with hopes of creating an hour-long scripted drama based on the book, the professional envy and tension between my husband and me worsened. Upon announcing the deal to my husband, with disdain, he said, "I've been working in this business since I was nine years old and no one has ever given me a development deal."

My entire career was built upon my computer. All the money I spent and everything he resented was made using that machine. He hated the idea that I didn't seem to try as hard as he did, yet was making more money than he was. Even now that he was a regular on a long-running soap, I was still the breadwinner. He hated my computer and all it represented, and now, it also held proof of his infidelity and proof that I wasn't the horrible person he made me out to be in the public and to his family. The emails I found were a sliver of truth that could damage the good ol' boy persona he was so desperate to hold on to. If anyone ever saw the emails, maybe, just maybe, I wouldn't seem so bad anymore.

Well, Aeron couldn't have that.

No one could know the truth about him and the life we lived, the torture and torment I withstood. All the evidence I needed to divorce and humiliate him was on that computer, along with everything I needed to continue to be successful.

My heart fell into my stomach when I realized that Aeron had, in fact, returned to the house after all and that he'd stolen my computer. Panicked, I scrambled for the phone, called the CBS lot where his soap opera was being filmed, and asked to speak to my husband, who, naturally, was not answering his mobile phone.

"Hi. This is Karrine, Aeron's wife. Has he reached set yet?"

"Aeron? I don't think he's on the schedule today. Let me double-check," the woman on the other end of the phone said. "No. Aeron isn't working today."

"Oh. Okay. Thanks."

And there it was.

It was just twelve days before Valentine's Day, 2010, and my husband's inappropriate sexual relationship with a 300-pound porn star had been revealed. He laughed at me when I confronted him with what I found, beat me with a belt in front of my son, and stole my computer containing all my work files and all the evidence I'd collected against him. He'd taken so much already but none of it was enough.

There was just one thing, though.

My computer backed up every hour on the hour, wirelessly, and all the information had already been stored. And, for insurance, I'd already printed out the emails between him and his fat fornicator. I may not have been strong enough to fight against him then, but I hoped that one day I would be and I wanted to gather as much evidence as I could. I immediately filed a restraining order against Aeron, citing the physical abuse over the last few years, and a theft report for my computer, knowing it was best for me to leave a paper trail. Unfortunately, Aeron was never in one spot long enough to have the restraining order served and there was no way to ever recover my computer.

A week later, the president of Fox Television Studios and my dear friend, David Madden, delivered a brand-new laptop to me so that I could finish the script I was writing for the company. I uploaded all the saved information from my wireless backup system and continued working as best I could while trying to find Aeron.

I called him constantly, leaving him voicemails and text messages several times a day. Eventually, just a few days before Valentine's Day, he answered.

"Yo," he said, sounding tired and stressed.

"Aeron, where is my computer?" I asked, skipping ridiculous pleasantries.

"I don't have your computer, Karrine."

"Really, Aeron? Where else could it be? We were the only people in the house. I left it on the couch when we went to bed and when I came back from taking Naiim to school, it was gone. Either you put it in your car before I got out of bed or you went back to the house and grabbed it after I left. Either way, I know you have it!"

"It was supposed to be a surprise."

"What was? Stealing my computer? Yeah! It was a surprise alright!"

"I was going to have it updated and give it back to you on Valentine's Day," he said, lazily. His voice drifted in and out as if he was half asleep or high.

"What the fuck are you talking about? None of that makes any sense. And where are you?" I asked, hearing people and commotion in the background.

"On a plane, headed to Vegas. Don't worry. Your precious computer is safe. You'll get it back. I've gotta go." And with that, Aeron hung up the phone.

Nearly a month would pass before I heard from him again.

On February 26, 2010, at nine o'clock on a rainy Friday night, a messenger appeared at my door with a very grand, very heavy bouquet of flowers at his feet and a manila envelope in his hands. I knew what was in it. It was inevitable. The messenger handed me the wet envelope, which had my initials scribbled on it in my husband's handwriting. Then, he handed me a clipboard and a pen so that I could sign for the receipt of the envelope and the papers inside.

Divorce papers.

I opened the envelope and peeked inside. My heart jumped and then fell. I grabbed the wet clipboard and pen from the messenger's hand and signed. He lifted the giant arrangement of flowers off the ground and asked where he should put them. Silently, I led him to the kitchen. Still stunned, I walked the stranger out, locked the front door, engaged the alarm, and walked back into the kitchen. I stared at the flowers and the divorce papers. With the flowers came a card with a message, written in Aeron's handwriting. It read, *I will always love you.*

Even now, he refused to stop torturing me.

Looking closely at the paperwork, I noticed it was signed and dated the day Aeron beat me with his belt and stole my computer, the day he lied about going to work. That day, after all he did to me, after all he took, he couldn't leave without taking just one more thing.

Everything.

CHAPTER THIRTEEN

Son of a Bitch

*I*t was March 2010 and I was in the midst of a serious bout of depression. I was unable to write anything and left the penning of my fourth book, *SatisFaction*, to a ghostwriter. My heart just wasn't in it. I lay around, listless, barely functioning, rarely eating or sleeping, smoking a pack of cigarettes a day and drinking alcohol by the case. I weighed just over 100 pounds and appeared gaunt and sickly. My hair was falling out, my nails turned yellow, and my face was covered in blotches and blemishes.

I felt my life was over.

Now, my marriage would be, too.

Aeron made sure he continued to torment me by sending me yet another large bouquet of flowers with a card reading, *Forever*, written and signed by him. Disgusted, I put the bouquet on the curb for a passerby to find, just as I had his first sickening set of divorce flowers. I was going through the worst time of my life and my husband was taunting me.

It was classic Aeron.

I felt like dying. I laid in bed all day, every day, crying and drinking alcohol. I'd done this for the majority of my years with Aeron, but, after the divorce filing, I seemed to sink further into my mattress and deeper into the bottom of the bottle. The house was quiet and dark and, as I hid away in my bedroom, my son hid away in his. The despair was palpable and infectious. I wanted to stop feeling like this. I wanted to be happy, and to me, that meant having my husband back. I just couldn't seem to understand that he was my sickness.

Somehow, in my mind, he was the remedy.

Coincidentally, about a week before I was served with the divorce papers, I had purchased a one-way airplane ticket for my friend Tanner to come to Los Angeles and stay with me while he took meetings around town and looked for work. I really needed the company and the support, and for the next seven weeks, Tanner stayed with me and gave me just that.

It was nice having someone in the house. Tanner was also in the midst of a tumultuous relationship and we found comfort in one another. He would read over my script for Fox and give me notes. We would venture out for breakfast at the local IHOP, as I began to gain my appetite back, and grab gourmet salads for lunch. We were both trying to take care of ourselves while reeling from our relationship woes. We binge-watched my favorite show, *The Tudors*, on demand, and soon it became his favorite show. We would just lay in bed with the curtains drawn and hold each other, staying far away from the outside world and everyone who hurt us.

But something was wrong.

From the day Tanner arrived during the first week of March, the energy surrounding his visit was off kilter. I woke up that morning, excited to pick him up from the airport. I prepared the guest room, making sure there were clean, crisp white towels and other accoutrements in his suite. While double-checking the room, I was met by a frantic bird tapping on the window. When I moved into the kitchen to wash a dish, that same frantic bird met me and began tapping on *that* window. For the next seven weeks during Tanner's visit, the bird came to the guest room window every morning and tapped worriedly until the sun went down. He would often come to the kitchen window when I was there and continue his tapping. Then, one day, weeks into Tanner's visit, the frantic little bird left the first-story guest room and kitchen windows and traveled down to the second story and to the completely opposite side of the house where my bedroom and bathroom windows were, and began tapping there as I brushed my teeth.

It was a sign.

Tanner always had a dark side to him, a demon he tried to keep hidden but one that escaped when he felt threatened. It seemed I was always attracting this sort of man and housing their energies. Even though he and I were just friends, he served as further proof of my propensity for chaos and destruction. I was always running from one bad man to another. By the end of his stay, Tanner's temper flared violently on two occasions, both times while we debated over random historical facts. He hated to be proven wrong. He was always very sensitive when it came to me, as he always insisted he was in love with me, but I could never return that love. This also frustrated him.

After a month, his friendly visit became strained and I began to wonder when he was leaving. I was ready to move on and to be alone. It seemed I could only attract violent, insecure men, and more than anything, I just wanted to be alone. I was exhausted and that poor nervous bird must have been exhausted, too. I didn't know how to tell Tanner it was time for him to go but I guess I didn't have to. Without saying a word, he packed his things and walked out the front door sometime in mid-April. He didn't say good-bye and I didn't care.

And the bird never returned.

By the time he left, I was ready for solitude and feeling stronger and healthier. Having company for almost two months helped me regain my appetite and much of the weight I lost over my time with Aeron. If Tanner served no other purpose, that was enough. I stopped drinking alcohol and smoking cigarettes and was more focused on my health and daily routine. I was more available to my son, in a better mood, and more involved.

We laughed more.

Even though I hadn't been successful at starting a new book since penning *The Vixen Manual* between 2007 and 2008, I was finding my stride in the world of television while writing the scripted version of that book. Even though I was being paid handsomely for creating the project, the money just wasn't enough. I was buried in debt while carrying a bill load of over $20,000 a month and struggling to hold on to the three-story, 6,000-square-foot home I acquired for my family—the family I never had.

Once Tanner left, it was as if someone took my training wheels off and I was coasting through my life all on my own for the first time in a while. However, I was finding it harder to recover professionally from the personal decisions I had made over the past three years. My relationship with Aeron had taken over my life and stolen my will to do anything. I hadn't worked as hard as I could have and was often a no-show at tour dates and events. Sickly and thin, I stayed out of the public eye and tried my best not to draw attention to myself as often as I once had. I'd lost a grip on my life and my will to live it. I suffered, my son suffered, and my work suffered. I was spending money at an alarming rate but hadn't done anything to ensure I made more money over a prolonged period. I'd spent the majority of the past three years in bed, crying and starving myself, popping anxiety medicine, and drinking.

But now that I seemed to be on the mend and had Aeron out of my life again, I was ready to get back to work. I began sending book proposals and ideas to my editor, only to be rejected over and over again before finally being released from my publishing contract altogether. For the first time in three years, I had no publishing home and no prospects. What I *did* have was the mountain of bills and debt I'd created as I tried to buy into the American Dream with a man who had no better intentions than to take advantage of me.

And then, Aeron came back.

Like clockwork, about two weeks after Tanner left, Aeron appeared at my door with Jonah in tow. It was that radar, his *she must be getting better* radar. She must be eating again. She must be getting back into a healthy routine. She must be okay without me. Let me go back and finish her off. Let me keep her down. And even though I would love to say that this is the part of the story where I slammed the door in his face and took control of my life, I can't. This is not that part. This is the part where I took Aeron back and tried to salvage my marriage. Not the marriage I had in real life—the marriage I had in my head. It was only May 2010, a little more than two months since Aeron served me with divorce papers, and I was already going back under.

For the next month, Aeron, the kids, and I fell into the perfect family routine. Jonah came into our room every morning at 7:30 to wake me. By this time, he'd stopped calling me *Mom*, at my request, and began calling me *Babe*, mimicking his father. I would make him a little morning snack, usually consisting of dried cereal or a breakfast bar with a glass of almond milk, before placing him back in bed to watch educational programming on television. While the baby was enjoying his snack, I'd hop into my son's room and begin getting him ready for school. While Naiim showered and prepared for his day, I would trot upstairs to get breakfast prepared. Aeron was usually just waking up around this time and would help me finish getting the boys ready and breakfast served before we all sat down and ate as a family. Then, Aeron would drive Naiim to school. We had a routine in place and our family soon functioned like a well-oiled machine.

In that first month, Aeron was home every day and our disagreements didn't turn violent. It seemed he was making a serious effort to change and be the husband and father I'd always needed him to be. We were actually getting along, and though you would think this would make everyone around us happy, it didn't, and no one was unhappier than Mona.

She had showed herself to be a vindictive, jealous woman over the years I'd spent with Aeron, and her jealousy and vindictiveness weren't just aimed at me, but at her son for being with me. I was under attack from all sides, with not one ally in the family into which I married. Though they all knew Mona was wicked, no one dared speak up against her and she made sure no one had a single, solitary pleasant thought about me. After all, I wasn't her daughter-in-law; I was her competition.

I remember early one rainy Thursday morning in 2008, during a sliver of time when Aeron and I were happy together, Mona had called.

"Hello?" I answered, as I nestled my head in Aeron's chest.

"Let me speak to my son," Mona barked, seeming emotionally unsound.

I handed the phone to Aeron. "It's your mom."

"What's up, Mom?" he asked as he put the phone to his ear.

Crying, Mona belted out, "It's raining and I can't take out the trash!"

"What do you mean you can't take out the trash?"

"It's raining!"

"Okay, but what does that have to do with the garbage, Mom?"

"I'm all alone and I don't have anybody to take the trash can to the curb for me," she whined, wailing into the phone. Lying on Aeron's chest, I could hear Mona going on and on about everyone leaving her, no one loving her, and not having anyone to help her do anything, ever. Never mind the fact that Aeron, his siblings, and their children were always over there, even living there for the majority of the time. At that point, though, everyone had moved out and Aeron was with me and she needed her son, or rather, her emotional husband. Riddling Aeron with guilt, Mona cried and cried until he got out of bed, into his car, out into the rain, and proceeded to drive over one hour to her house, just to take her trash can to the curb.

I didn't see him again for over a week.

Mona was always doing something to pull Aeron away from me when we were getting along and keeping him away from me when we weren't. She never urged him to do the right things. She celebrated him, even and especially when he was at his worst. She coddled him and called him a king, even though everything he did in life pointed to the contrary. As long as he came home to her and not to me, she was satisfied.

There was a period of many months, also back in 2008, when Aeron hadn't received any residual checks from any of his previous work over the past twenty years. We were trying to work things out and I was insisting he contribute to the household bills. He promised he would, as soon as he got his checks. He was struggling to make it, as usual, and all of his expenses were falling on me. I was stressed. Aeron was stressed. But Mona wasn't stressed at all. She said she was making money in her candle-making business, though every time we visited her, her display of candles never seemed to be disturbed or diminished. I confided in her about Aeron and my financial issues often and she always seemed sympathetic. Mona took the opportunity to rescue him every time I complained, offering the money he needed for his personal bills and debt, leaving me to continue to carry the large sum of bills and expenses in the household. When she called, he ran to her and would stay for days or for a week or two as she baited him.

Months passed and Aeron continued to wonder where his residual checks could be, as did I. He would call Mona every week and ask if they arrived, and she would always say, "No." The pressure was mounting. So, finally, I called a friend who worked at the Screen Actors Guild, in the payments department, and asked him when Aeron was due to be paid. Come to find out, Aeron's residual checks had been issued on time and in the sum of about $10,000 and sent to the mailbox address he shared with his mother. Not only that, someone had cashed them. (Aeron had since opened a new account separate from his mother, as he tried to gain some sort of financial independence.) When I brought this to Aeron's attention, he claimed to not know anything about it.

Mona's goal always seemed to be to place more stress on our relationship and to propel Aeron right back into his mother's bosom. There was the time Mona kept Aeron at her place for over a week, claiming she needed help moving out of her house since neither she nor Aeron could afford the mortgage, bills, and upkeep of the home. He spent his birthday with his mother instead of with me, and stayed for over a week until Mother's Day morning. It was Sunday, May 11,

2008, when Aeron finally came home, sometime around 6 AM. He'd obviously had to sneak out of his mother's house before she awoke. After his hour-long drive, he crawled into bed with me and settled down to rest. We may have dozed off for about an hour before the phone rang. Without even looking at the Caller ID, I already knew who was calling—I had been waiting for the fallout.

"Hello?" I said, as I answered the phone.

"You fucking bitch! Put my fucking son on the phone, you fucking bitch!" Mona screamed on the other end of the line.

Calmly, I removed the phone from my ear and handed it to Aeron. "Here; your mother's on the phone."

I could hear Mona continue to yell through the phone as Aeron tried to calm her down. "Whoa, whoa, hold up, Mom! What's wrong with you?"

"How are you going to leave me to go be with that bitch? You want to be with her? Then, fine! Be with her and don't come back over here!" Mona screamed, sounding more like a jilted wife than a mother.

In what I overheard, Mona continued to berate me and chastise him just for wanting to spend some alone time with me on Mother's Day before taking her out to dinner later that evening. Within minutes, Aeron was out the door and headed back to his mother's house. I didn't see him for another three days.

Incidents like these were plenty and often. Mona rarely missed a chance to pretend to be a concerned mother-in-law and *never* missed a chance to sabotage me, either directly or indirectly. She was a miserable, vicious woman who loved her son inappropriately and fed the monster within him. She always patted his head when he did well and when he did wrong, and stripped him of his emotional and financial independence when she felt he wasn't doing enough for her. Aeron was always spirited by many demons—one of them being his mother. After all, it was she who raised him to be the person he became.

But, of all Mona's tricks and menacing ways, the worst was yet to come.

CHAPTER FOURTEEN

With a Vengeance

Since Aeron returned home in May 2010, we managed to continue our routine and stave away any major arguments or physical fights as he continued to work on the soap opera and make a steady income. Aeron didn't contribute much to the household but he did what he could. For maybe the second time in our entire three-year relationship, we celebrated Mother's Day together, and for the first time, Aeron invited me to join him at a red carpet event. Though our divorce was still moving forward, we seemed to be on the mend and working toward having the family I always wished we would. I also wished he would withdraw the divorce but there was never any talk of it. I didn't want to rock the boat.

Aeron asked me to go with him to the Thirty-Seventh Annual Daytime Emmy Awards in Las Vegas that June just two days before the award show, and frankly, it seemed as if he didn't really want me to go. Though he claimed he invited me to prove to me he was a changed man, in retrospect, it was more about inviting my wallet than it was about inviting me. Still, I was thrilled to finally be included in something and scurried to get the children all packed and ready to spend a few days with Mona while Aeron and I took the trip along with his brother, Jonathan, and his girlfriend.

We left Los Angeles and made the three-hour drive to Las Vegas in my Range Rover. I paid for the gas. Once we arrived, Aeron and I checked into the Trump International Hotel. I paid for the room. We ate and drank at the hotel's prestigious restaurant and at other hotels on the famed Las Vegas Strip. I paid for that, too. A day before the event, Aeron unpacked a leather suit he must have purchased back in the early nineties; he always had the worst style and tended to dress like an old man from an era far gone. I took one look at the suit and drove him to the Hugo Boss at the mall to get a more updated, debonair suit, tailored to fit his large, broad frame. He also needed appropriate underwear, socks, a pocket square, and shoes.

I paid for it all.

The trip to Las Vegas wasn't perfect, since we had a few major fallouts during our days there, but overall we made the best of the trip and had a good time. This obviously bothered Mona as she called to complain about every little thing she could. After living in Los Angeles for decades, Mona still called Aeron for directions to just about everywhere around town. If she lost something around the house, she called him. If she had a question about something to which she already knew the answer, she called him. Aeron would often take his mother with him to events, and it bothered her that he was attending this event with me in Las Vegas while she was stuck at home with our kids as well as his brother's two children. Mona was feeling left out and did everything she could to ruin our trip all the way from Los Angeles by calling often and always with a supposed problem none of us could solve from Las Vegas.

It was typical Mona.

Still, we survived the trip, made the very best of it, and drove back to Los Angeles two days after the Emmys only to return to Las Vegas a week later for a bit of personal time. Again, we left the kids with Mona, and though she did her best to pretend to be happy to sit with the children while Aeron and I continued to get along and rebuild our relationship, she was fuming and I knew it. However, it would take another month for me to find out just how angry, jealous, and vengeful Mona could be.

As the summer went on, Aeron and I continued to rebuild and dedicate our personal time to each other and the children. He was spending a lot less time with his mother, and he wasn't depending on her to help him with Jonah anymore and was leaving him at home with me instead. In mid-July, when Jonah's third birthday rolled around, Aeron and I spent the day alone with the children and had our own little party—just the four of us.

Mona was irate.

She called and complained to Aeron about not spending time with her grandson and being left out of his birthday celebration. Though her complaints were understandable, Aeron was making a clear statement that he was trying to build his own family and start his own traditions with our children and me and that everything he did in his life didn't have to include his mother. He was trying to send her a message and trying to prove to me that we were a family, our own unit, separate from his bat-shit crazy mother and other members of their family. But Mona would have none of it. She argued with Aeron, making him feel guilty for spending the day with his wife and children, berating him until he agreed to bring the baby over to her house the following day, which he did. But, still trying to cut the cord between him and his mother, he left soon after dropping Jonah off at Mona's and came back home to be with me.

It was obvious when Aeron returned that he was annoyed by a conversation he had with his mother while at her house. He began to explain, "I just don't know what to do about her. She's so ridiculous."

"Your mother is jealous, Aeron," I chimed.

"I know. She's always been this way. She's one of the main reasons none of my relationships have ever worked out. She never wanted to see me with anybody but her."

"That's because you're her husband and you've been her husband since your father left."

"I'm not her husband! Eew!"

"Yeah. It sounds gross because it is. Doesn't make it untrue."

"But even with you. She'll do whatever she can to keep me away from you. Do you know she tried to convince me that my son told her you hurt him?"

"Hurt him? What do you mean hurt him?"

"She says that he told her you slapped him on his penis."

My heart dropped, my stomach turned, and my blood boiled. "She said what? When the fuck did she say this?"

"About a month ago, right after we got back from Las Vegas."

"And what the fuck did you say? What did you do?"

"Well, I asked him about it and he said you've never hurt him, that he loves you and you're his Babe. So, I left it at that."

"And you never once thought to tell me about this?"

"I really didn't want to make a big deal about it because I know it's not true."

I began pacing the floor, my breaths shallow and quick. "I am so sick of your mother! I have taken her shit for *three* years without saying one cross word to her! The *one* Thanksgiving we spent together, she yelled at me for giving you a peck on the lips and said it was inappropriate! I said *nothing* to her. Just before you came back home this last time, she called me to tell me my 'little success ain't shit' even though my *little success* has taken care of you and her grandson for years! And I *still* said nothing! All the snide comments and back-stabbing, telling me no one likes me and acting like she's bringing me into the fold when, in actuality, she's been making *sure* no one likes me! And when she had me pulled over by the sheriff's department after telling them I was driving around, suicidal, with my son in the car, just because I called her crying after we broke up! And you know she's running around telling your family I hurt that little boy! You know she is!"

"Calm down. I'll handle it."

"Handle it? Have you been handling it? This has been going on a month and this is the first time I'm hearing about it! I'm calling her. Fuck that! I'm tired of that bitch and I'm tired of being nice and trying to keep the peace when all she does is try to destroy me."

"Don't. Don't do that. I'll take care of it!"

Livid, I grabbed the phone, feverishly dialed Mona's number, and before she could even say hello, I started in on her. With intensity and blatant disregard, I told that woman everything I thought about her, everything I loathed about her, and gave her hell for the way she'd treated me for the past three years. I spoke to her the way she deserved and held nothing back. I was done being abused by her. Her claims about me were outrageous, dangerous, and threatened everyone's lives. An accusation this powerful could cause authorities to rip the children from our home and send me to jail—and she'd made it only because her son was with me and not with her. The obvious irony of it all was that Mona had friends and family members in the Los Angeles Sheriff's Department, and Mona was awarded some sort of honorary social services badge, which she loved to wave around as a threat every time my son showed up with a bruise or a cut from the school playground. She accused me of assaulting her grandchild's genitals, yet didn't act to have me arrested or even investigated. Of course not, because none of it was true; it was all just another ploy to get her son away from me and back with her.

For years, I'd been like an abused animal with my tail tucked, huddled in a corner, shaken and afraid. I was taking abuse from strangers all over the world, from my husband, and even from his mother. Everywhere I turned, no one validated or celebrated my successes or me. Instead, I was always being told I wasn't good enough, that I wasn't worthy, and that no one wanted me. My husband even told me once, "There is no one else in the world that would marry you."

And I believed him.

This was my life!

Every single day, I was being punished, beaten, and put upon. Looking back on it all, I don't know how I survived it. I don't know how I didn't just blow my fucking brains out. And, on that day, the day I finally exploded and told Mona everything I'd been burying, something changed inside of me and everything changed in my relationship with my mother-in-law.

I untucked my tail, I showed my teeth, and I bit.

I was proud of myself and felt a ton rolling off my shoulders. I had just put Mona on alert that I would no longer stand for her foolishness, her meddling, and her accusations. I put my foot down, stood my ground, and Mona seemed to have a newfound respect for me. She may have been someone's mother, but she wasn't *my* mother. I was not her child, so I would no longer allow her to treat, talk to, or chastise me as if I were. I was slowly unraveling the ties that bound me, and even though there was a lot more fraying to be done, it began that day. As I reveled in the erection of my spine, Aeron walked out the door and headed back to his mother's side, shaming me for standing up to her in a way he never could—jealous of my freedom.

And there it was.

That was it, all along.

It was my freedom—my unabashed way of living, of being, of running through life unapologetically with no one to answer to and no one telling me where to go, what time to be there, and how to behave when I arrived. I was my own boss. I owned my life. That was what Aeron was attracted to in me and this is what he wanted to destroy.

That was what I *let* him destroy.

Now, things were changing.

But neither he nor his mother would let me be free, again.

Not without a fight.

CHAPTER FIFTEEN

The Unraveling

By August 2010, my marriage to Aeron was legally over, and after my argument with his mother, Aeron stayed away for the most part, coming and going as he pleased. We were right back to our old habits and the cycle of abuse continued. But that November, when Aeron invited me to join him at a listening party he was holding for the album he'd been working on since forever, I wanted to support him. He knew I never believed in his dream of becoming a musician and even though his voice was beautiful, he'd always been dated and uncool. He just didn't have *it*. I was accustomed to running around with the crème of the musical crop and his incessant need to be an artist was embarrassing to me. To put it plainly, Aeron was just corny.

But he was just as obsessive about his music as I was about our relationship. So, I continued to vie for his approval by showing mine. I was excited to join him that night and rushed to pick up Naiim from school, shower, change, and meet Aeron at the Sunset Marquis Hotel in West Hollywood. There, just off the parking garage, is a recording studio they call Nightbird.

I walked into the studio and felt all eyes on me. I was still uncomfortable around people and was never good at making new friends, especially when everyone in the room was already judging me based on what they thought they knew about me.

Aeron saw me as I walked in and greeted me. "Hey, you want a drink?" he asked as he showed me to a seat in the far corner of the room.

"Yeah. Sure! Is there white wine?" I asked, being mindful to stay upbeat and smile in the presence of strangers. I sat in the seat Aeron appointed for me and waited for him to bring my drink. He left the studio and returned several minutes later with two drinks in his hand, neither of them a glass of wine. He walked in laughing with one of his friends before making eye contact with another woman who was sitting closer to the door. He handed her one of the drinks he held and stood next to her as they both began sipping their cocktails.

I just sat there.

Aeron never brought me that glass of wine, so eventually I stormed out of the studio and headed for the hotel's outdoor bar. There, I met a couple of other patrons, struck up a conversation, watched the ball game playing on the television above the bar, and bought my own glass of wine. I must have been out there for over an hour and never once did Aeron call or text to see where I'd gone. I began to wonder why he even bothered inviting me to the event if he only intended to ignore me the entire night. I wondered—until I realized that *was* the reason he invited me.

By the time I made my way back toward the recording studio with the intent to get in my car and go home, I was tipsy and furious. As I made my way past the studio and toward the valet, I ran into Aeron, who coyly cackled as a woman draped herself over his shoulders. Aeron was a flirt and he never saw anything wrong with his overtly inappropriate dealings with women, whether in public or in private. He didn't see the implications of it when he took those two women to the *Why Did I Get Married* premiere or when he carried on a relationship with an overweight sex-worker. It was all fun and games to him and it was all torture to me.

"Get the fuck off my husband," I demanded as I charged the woman, removing her arm from his neck.

"Oh! I'm sorry," she responded, genuinely shocked and bewildered. "I didn't know you had a wife," she continued, turning to Aeron in search of answers.

"What the fuck is wrong with you," Aeron growled. "That's my sister's neighbor. She's like family and I'm not your husband!"

I'd forgotten about our divorce. Aeron and I were still involved, still having sex, still sharing a bed, and he still inhabited my home when he felt the need, but he was no longer my husband.

"Family? Family doesn't act the way she's acting—the way the both of you are acting!" I belligerently rebutted. Plus, I recognized her. Back when I found the disturbing string of emails between Aeron and Felicia Fats, I also came across other inappropriate or suggestive emails and photos from several other women. This woman was one of them.

Before the situation could escalate, Aeron grabbed me by my forearm and pulled me toward the valet, ordering them to bring my car around. By this time, all his guests had poured out into the parking garage and stood idly by as Aeron and I began to argue. We shouted at each other as the valet scurried to deliver my car. As the Mercedes pulled up behind me, the valet opened the car door and left it that way. Aeron and I walked and argued until I stood in the open doorway, my back to the car. The argument became more and more heated and, true to form, Aeron pushed his large forearm into my chest and tried to force me into the car. I hit my head on the doorframe as I resisted his push. He grabbed my neck and continued to push me into the car as I fought back, screaming, begging him to let go of me.

Everyone watched.

No one helped.

I could taste blood in my mouth as the altercation continued. Eventually, one of Aeron's friends pulled him off me and ordered him into his car. I scrambled for my phone and called the police as I watched Aeron and his friend flee the scene. Over the next fifteen minutes, while I waited for the West Hollywood police to respond, the hotel's management ordered everyone else to leave the premises. All the witness left—all except for one man who stayed with me as I waited for the police in the hotel's lobby. When the officers arrived, they took photos and video evidence of my bruises and helped me begin the process of obtaining a restraining order against my ex-husband. They asked if I needed an ambulance and I refused. Battered and broken, I just wanted to go home, curl up into a ball, and die.

Over the next several weeks, I did everything I could to build a case against Aeron. Initially, I was determined to fight back the only way I could—in court. I wanted to prove once and for all that I wasn't the bad one in this relationship. I wanted to be vindicated against all the horrible things he said about me and all the lies he told people about our relationship. I wanted the world to see him hitting, pushing, and choking me. And all I needed was the hotel's surveillance footage.

I visited the Sunset Marquis on two separate occasions after the incident to speak to the hotel's manager, who was of no help to me. I asked if I could have a copy of the footage and was refused. I was told there was no footage, that there were no cameras in the underground parking garage where guests kept their expensive, luxury vehicles. I was told lies. No one wanted to help me. No one cared and I went back home, defeated once again.

In my mind, I'd already resigned myself to the fact that Aeron was eventually going to kill me and there was nothing I could do about it. So, on November 22, 2010, I wrote a letter to those I'd known professionally and personally and sent it to everyone on my contact list. I figured I would write the letter then, so that when they found me dead, they would know who did it and that I knew it was coming but had been too sick to stop it.

Domestic Violence: An Open Letter

I've been a victim of abuse all my life—literally, for as long as I can remember. It is my norm. Whereas most people would run in the other direction the moment someone physically, emotionally, or mentally abused them—I stay.

It's a sickness and just when I think I am cured, the cancer spreads.

For the past several years, I have been involved in a highly abusive relationship. I have been choked, whipped with belts, thrown about, berated, belittled, raped, and disregarded as a human being. I have been abandoned and embarrassed, then loved and coddled.

I have been caught in a vicious cycle and have left on many occasions, just to return. I have found little support from my friends and family because I complain and I cry, then I go back for more. I go back knowing that, one day, he'll kill me, but he's all I have. He's the only one who understands because he's stuck in this cycle, too.

When I try to confide in friends, they ask, "Well, what did you do to him? What did you say to him?" They tell me, "You know how he is, he's never going to change, so why do you stay? You know what you're getting into. Don't tell anyone because he'll come out looking good and you'll only make yourself look bad." It's always my fault.

No one understands—not even me.

So, I keep it all to myself and it continues. Then, we make up and vow it will never happen again—then it does and I feel so foolish for ever believing he can change or that we can change. Then, I begin to believe again. I believe even now.

I love him though it pains me to admit.

It sickens me to know that I will return to him in an instant and that the next time could be the last time and that breath, my last breath. Still, I hold out hope that one day we'll learn how to love one another without pain. I pray that those who look on with smirks and judgments know one thing—domestic violence is very real and, at times, very final.

If you, or someone you know, has been a victim of domestic violence, please contact the National Domestic Abuse Hotline at (800) 799-7233.

I was dying and reaching out for help.

My letter reached a friend who worked with the producers of the *Dr. Phil Show,* and soon I was on the phone with one of the show's producers, explaining my relationship and the abuse that plagued it since the beginning. Naturally, they wanted us on the show and I was just desperate enough to do it, if it meant I could shine a light on what was really happening in my relationship and in my life and if it meant that Aeron and I could receive some sort of help or that I could get away. I felt I would be better protected if more people knew—if the world knew. But, of course, when the producers contacted Aeron, he was not interested in the attention. He didn't want anyone to know about the documented abuse and injuries I suffered at his hand and, without his participation, the producers of the *Dr. Phil Show* decided I wasn't worth helping. Shortly afterward, sometime in December of 2010, Aeron wrote to me via email, *It doesn't matter who you tell. No one cares about you anymore. No one wants to hear anything from you anymore.* And that was all he wanted, for no one to care about me. He resented my very existence and would have done anything to see it plagued or even ended.

From my computer, I watched as gossip blogs made up stories about me, belittled and berated me, lying about my being involved with men and women I'd never even met, perpetuating the constant slut shaming I had endured since the onset of my career. I watched the world spin a fictitious web around me and the persona I created, and when a story leaked about the abuse I suffered at Aeron's hands, it was reported that I deserved it.

I must have.

No one ever cared about me. No one ever loved me. I never had anywhere to go and no one to save me or help me. All I'd ever done was be honest about my life, who I was, who I wanted to be, where I wanted to go and my journey to that place, wherever it is. I never lied, not even about my worst mistakes, and I never made anyone look worse than I did. But I am a woman, and therefore my life is valued less than that of a dog's.

This is what the world taught me.

And I couldn't fight the world. I didn't have the energy to order cease and desists on every blog and magazine that posted or printed scathing, defamatory falsities. I couldn't stand up for myself in public—I was too busy trying to save my life in private.

Naturally, Aeron and I did not spend the 2010 holiday season together. But soon he and I would make amends and jump back into our vicious cycle. He continued to creep in and out of the house at his leisure whenever he wanted something.

And, as always, I was there to give it to him.

But I was finally nearing the end of my tether.

There never seemed to be a time I didn't begin and end my day in tears. I was sick of living this way but was in too deep to see my way out. Once again, I found it hard to eat and I began drinking too much. I spent most of my days in bed or perched on the balcony just outside my bedroom's back door, smoking cigarettes and ignoring phone calls from concerned friends, like Deneen. I'd been ready for a change for years and didn't have the esteem, but now I would be forced to make changes because I was running out of money—and fast.

By New Year's Day 2011, it was all over. There was only enough money in my accounts for one more rent payment, an astounding $6,000, and I wasn't expecting another check until April. There was no way I could survive in that house for another three months and had no choice but to leave. I slept through New Year's Eve and most of New Year's Day, feeling listless and despondent, and then, on January 2, I awoke with a new resolve.

We were leaving.

With a fire I hadn't known in years, I sprang out of bed and ran out my bedroom for the first time in days. I barged into Naiim's room and announced, "Start packing; we're moving." He looked at me in confusion and, then, with a sense of relief. "I'm tired of everyone going about their lives and we're just stuck here, watching them come and go. Everyone is having fun and living life and it's like we're living in a prison. So, let's start by making a pile of things we're not taking with us and throwing those things out. I'll grab the empty boxes from the garage."

Naiim didn't hesitate.

This move was a long time coming.

Leaving the house, the mausoleum, the shrine I created and kept up all in the name of pulling a family together out of a million broken pieces, was more than a change of venue—it was an escape from Aeron. I started looking for apartments on the other side of town, out of the hilly suburbs and in the bustling city about thirty minutes away. I didn't want to live in that neighborhood anymore; I didn't want to see the same streets, restaurants, and stores Aeron and I visited over the past five years. It seemed as if every building within a ten-mile radius had a memory attached to it and I wanted no part of any of them.

In a flurry, I packed up the house and made arrangements for my furniture broker to buy back the majority of the furniture that filled its three stories. In the end, he bought over $30,000 worth of furniture for just $3,000—money I desperately needed. Even then, I still had to borrow money from friends to pay for the costs of moving and closing out my bills and the lease at my current home. I even got Aeron to shell out a few hundred bucks and pack a few boxes, the few times he came by to visit. Whenever he inquired as to where Naiim and I would be moving, I always told him I wasn't sure and that I was still waiting to be approved for a place. It was never my intention to let him know where we'd be or to let him back into our lives once we moved.

I was looking forward to a new start.

Scared but looking forward.

The most difficult part of leaving the old neighborhood had to be pulling Naiim out of school and away from his friends. Even though he loved our home, he was ready to move on from what it represented and the energy that lived there. What he wasn't ready to do was change his life completely and move into the city for the first time in his nearly thirteen years. Sure, we could have easily stayed in the suburbs. God knows it would have been a lot easier and cheaper, but I couldn't bear the thought of wallowing in the same town for one more day.

I really just wanted to be happy.

I really just wanted to be free.

So, with our bravest faces painted on, Naiim and I walked through his school, getting all his teachers to sign him out of their classes, returning his textbooks and turning in the last of his assignments. All his friends, many of whom he'd known since kindergarten, wished him good luck and told him good-bye. He was so strong and I knew he was doing it for me. But the moment we got back in the car and shut the doors, my son broke down and sobbed.

Tears flooded from my eyes as my son grieved the life he was leaving behind and questioned the life ahead. I held onto him and tried my best to assure him that we would be okay, that the move would be tough but that it was necessary for us to start completely over.

"I'm so sorry, Naiim," I said as I held my son, kissing his face. "I know this isn't easy but we have to do it; we have to move on with our lives and try something new. This place is killing me and that's hurting you. Just think of it as a new adventure, a new life for us— just you and me. I promise, I'll make everything okay."

As I dried his tears, I hoped my son believed me; I hoped he trusted me, and more than anything, I hoped everything I told him was true. I didn't know what was going to happen next. I didn't yet know where we would end up and if anything I was doing would be the right thing. All I knew was that I'd fucked up our lives and I wanted to fix them.

I searched for the right apartment in just the right neighborhood, with an appropriate rent and a feasible move-in cost. I called around and visited a few properties until finding the perfect one, and by January 14, Naiim and I were moved out of the prison we inhabited and settled into our new apartment—all without telling Aeron where we were headed. By that time, after years of carrying such a heavy financial burden, my credit was shot. And between the closing bills at the house, the move-in costs at the new place, the price of the movers, and the storage needed to keep things that didn't fit into the tiny 1,250-square-foot apartment, I was all out of money. Still, Naiim and I were headed to our new home and a new chance at life. I was finally going to start over and make right all the bad decisions I'd made since 2007.

I was exhausted during the last night of the move and happy to be just three blocks from my new place with the last set of boxes piled into my Mercedes. Behind me, one of the movers was driving my SUV, also packed with boxes, while the other two trailed behind in the moving van. Naiim and I were almost home. Driving on a busy city street, lined with restaurants and night clubs, we whizzed past one of many valet stands when suddenly a parking attendant opened a car door wide, hitting the passenger-side rearview mirror of my car, snapping it.

This was the last thing I needed.

I'd recently made arrangements to return both my cars to the dealers, unable to afford the $3,000 monthly in payments. I was trying to simplify my life and downsizing was the first step. But now, with the mirror broken, there was no way I could return the car and incur the outrageous dealership fees from having their technicians fix the damages. It would cost me less to have the mirror fixed myself, but I couldn't even afford cheap labor at that point. I tried for the next couple of weeks to raise the money, to no avail, and I was just weeks away from having to return the car to the dealership.

I needed help, and every time I felt vulnerable, I always reached for Aeron. I tried so hard not to do it this time. I tried so hard to depend on someone else, but after shutting myself away from the world for so long, there was no one I could call.

Desperate, I called Aeron.

It was a bad decision and I knew that as I was making it. Moving was my first real attempt at leaving Aeron and my life with him behind and I fucked it all up. I was so different from that girl who drove herself to the emergency room that I didn't know who I was anymore. He was all I knew at that point and as much as I wanted a life without him, I didn't know how to go about getting it.

Aeron was happy to come to my rescue. I sent him directions to my new apartment via email and, anxious to know where I'd moved, he came right over. A few days and six hundred dollars later, the mirror was fixed, and even though he was the one who paid for the repairs, I was the one paying the heftiest price.

It was February 2, 2011, and Aeron was back in my life.

CHAPTER SIXTEEN

Order of Protection

*I*t didn't take long for Aeron and me to fall back into our destructive routine. Naturally, not having had sufficient time apart, nothing changed after I moved out of the house. We were both still playing a game of cat and mouse, pretending we were leaving one another, saying we were done, but pulling each other back into the pit that had become so comfortable to us over the years. He picked up right where he left off, making promises he had no intention of keeping and disregarding my feelings, and I continued my efforts to somehow fix our relationship. Though our marriage was over and I had grown to be okay with that, I still hoped we could be cordial and loving toward one another and stop tearing our children apart. The two boys had grown close during their years together and continued to refer to one another as brothers. But Aeron just couldn't help himself. He continued to be abusive and dismissive and I continued to accept it.

But things were changing all around us and inside of me.

Jonah's mother had been on a campaign to regain custody of him since about a year after foolishly signing what she believed to be a temporary custody agreement. With the help of her parents, she opened a child-custody case in a Chicago court and began the fight to get Jonah back. By now, she was married and living in a home her father purchased for the newlyweds, Jonah, and her new husband's children from a previous relationship. She wanted her family to be together and I couldn't blame her. I understood how necessary it was to have a family and to have that family be complete.

Jonah's mother and her parents stopped at nothing to bring him back home to Chicago. They delved into Aeron's past and were having him surveilled as he went about his days in Los Angeles. They interviewed people who knew Aeron and had been around during the past few years as he reared Jonah, including me. During my conversations with Jonah's family in Chicago, I found out things about Aeron I never knew, and for the first time in five years, I refused to protect him. I told them everything I'd seen—things that would horrify any mother.

Aeron was never the ideal father, though no one could ever tell him he wasn't doing it properly. He was oddly obsessed with Michael Jackson and had it in his head that Jonah's mother was just a carrier from whom he was justified in purchasing his child, the way he assumed Michael Jackson had done with his children. He carried his son with him everywhere he went, treating Jonah more like an accessory than a person. This poor baby was being dragged to early-morning and late-night meetings and was walking around dangerous television and film sets, sleeping in trailers and in green rooms. Though I always begged Aeron to leave Jonah at home with me so that Jonah could get proper nutrition, care, and rest, Aeron mostly refused. The times when he did feel it appropriate to leave the child with someone else, he would drop Jonah off at Mona's for days or weeks at a time, or at his sister's, brother's, or various friends' homes. All the while, Jonah craved stability and a sense of normalcy.

Just like I did.

Aeron didn't really live anywhere when he wasn't living with me. He didn't have his own place and slept at this house and that, with family and friends. For a time, before they moved, Jonathan, his girlfriend, and their daughter all lived with Mona. When the couple had another daughter, the four-bedroom house became full. Still, Aeron and Jonah claimed to live there as well, as Aeron tried his best to appear stable to Jonah's mother. However, the fact that Aeron and Jonah were forced to share a bedroom in the overly occupied home didn't fare well with Jonah's mother.

None of the information I shared with Jonah's family, nor the information they found while investigating Aeron, made them comfortable, and after months of compiling proof against Aeron, they decided it was time to call Los Angeles's child protection agency to see about the living conditions to which Aeron was subjecting Jonah. I wasn't aware they'd done so until after the fact, when Jonah's grandmother in Chicago told me. Although the move was something I understood, and a necessary one on their part, I knew all too well there would be consequences for going against Aeron.

Late one afternoon in April, two days after Jonah's family called Child Protective Services, there was a thunderous knock on my door. Looking out the peephole, I saw three police officers positioned to pounce, their hands on their weapons. Behind them was a thin Hispanic man holding a clipboard. My first thought was that there was an emergency in the building. I thought that maybe there was a murderer or rapist on the loose and the authorities were here with a property manager to secure the premises. That had to be it; they couldn't be there for me.

Except they were.

"Are you Karrine Steffans?" the man with the clipboard asked once I opened the door, my heart pounding nervously in my chest. The three police officers stood at the ready, their hands still on the butt of their pistols, as the man made his way through the wall of officers and to my front door.

"Yes. What's going on?" I responded, growing more nervous and afraid by the second.

"My name is Roberto Fernandez and I am an agent with the Department of Children and Family Services for the county of Los Angeles. I am here, accompanied by officers of the Los Angeles Police Department, because DCFS has received an anonymous tip. May we come in?"

"Sure," I said as I moved to the side, allowing the four of them to enter the apartment. I tried my best to remain calm as my anxiety began to turn to anger. I knew exactly who had done this.

"Who else is in the home?" asked one of the officers.

"Just my son," I promptly replied, pointing to his closed bedroom door.

"Do you mind if we take a look around?"

"No. Go ahead."

As the officers took the very brief tour of my tiny apartment, Agent Fernandez began to explain the details of the anonymous tip he received. "The caller claimed you were running a brothel out of your home, subjecting your son to the presence of the men coming in and out of the home. The caller alleged you are abusing heroin, as well as physically and emotionally abusing your son, leaving him alone for weeks at a time and not feeding him for days."

"I know who did this," I responded, shaking my head and smirking just a bit. "Sir, I am on the tail end of a five-year abusive relationship with my ex-husband. This man has also been abusive to his child, and the mother of that child just called your department to report him two days ago. I'm sure he thinks I either did it or had some part in it and this is his way of getting back at me." As I continued to talk, the officers excused themselves and exited the apartment after assessing there was no immediate danger to the agent.

"So, you're saying all these allegations are false and were made as a form of retaliation from your ex-husband?"

"Yes, sir."

"And there is an open case against him with the Department of Children and Family Services?"

"Yep. It was just opened the other day. I can give you all the information and show you a paper trail documenting the abuse I have endured over the past five years, including battery and injury reports, all the temporary restraining orders I have had against him, and the attempts I have made to make those temporary orders permanent, to no avail."

"Why haven't you been able to make them permanent?"

"Because I can never find him. He doesn't live anywhere and moves around a lot. He's never had a steady job until now, and it's impossible to have him served at the CBS lot; no one can get past security. So I can never protect myself and he keeps coming back."

"And you're sure he's the one making these allegations against you?"

"Either him or his mother, yes. But he's the only person who knows where I live. I just moved into this apartment two months ago and he's the only person who's been here. Plus, he's always tried to make me look like a bad mother. He's always lied about me on every level, privately and publicly. He's done nothing but try to destroy me and my son since the moment I let him into my life. I guess now he's trying to finish me off for good." I started crying, knowing I had opened myself up to Aeron's hateful antics once again and I could be made to pay with my life and that of my innocent son.

Over the course of my conversation with the agent, I gathered all the evidence I had of the abuse I suffered at Aeron's hand and gave him Aeron's full name, as well Jonah's and that of Jonah's mother. I told him about all the years Aeron spent in court, trying to keep Jonah away from his mother and how she'd finally had enough. I told the agent about the surveillance and the damaging things Jonah's family in Chicago had found out about Aeron. I even told him about Mona and how she'd accused me of abusing Jonah and even Naiim—that this was their go-to maneuver, their first line of attack when trying to ruin my life. I painted a complete picture of the situation for Agent Fernandez and, by the end of our first meeting, he knew I wasn't the problem. He knew I wasn't the bad one and for the first time, I felt I had someone who believed me and wanted to protect me from the monster I once married.

It may have taken extreme circumstances, but I was glad to have someone in my corner. I was willing to go through whatever process the state needed if it meant they were going to help me protect myself against Aeron. He thought making these false reports against me would hurt me but his plan was backfiring.

"The first thing I need you to do is file a restraining order against your ex-husband, again, and I will help you serve him," Agent Fernandez instructed. "You have to do this as a measure of keeping you and your son safe and free from abuse. If the department feels you are not doing enough to keep your son safe from Aeron, *that* is considered abuse, as well. So, I'll help you do that."

He folded a sheet of paper in half and scribbled down a list of three other recommendations:

1. Domestic violence group counseling and/or education to help mother recognize her behaviors which place her at risk of witnessing abuse.
2. Individual therapy to address ongoing anxiety.
3. Conjoint therapy for mother and son.

Though Agent Fernandez believed my stories of emotional and physical abuse, there was nothing he could do to close the case Aeron opened against me. Once a case is opened in Los Angeles County, it cannot be closed until certain steps are taken and the state finds the case satisfactorily addressed.

Immediately, I filed a restraining order against Aeron—the third in five years—but this time, I had help getting it served. Agent Fernandez and the Los Angeles Police Department used social media to find out where Aeron would be and sat outside a local venue where he and his brother were scheduled to perform. I stayed by the phone that night as Agent Fernandez called me frequently with updates from his car outside the venue. Finally, as I dozed off on the sofa, I received one final call.

"He's been served," Agent Fernandez reported.

"Oh my God! Thank you! Thank you! Thank you!" I exclaimed, delighted to know I'd finally been able to take the step needed to protect myself against Aeron. Aeron's restraining order against me, which he'd filed back in 2008, was still valid, but neither of us had been adhering to it. Even when I asked Aeron to stay away, he wouldn't, even though *he* was the one who filed the order. I was tired of this sick cycle and after he made such disgusting claims against me with the Department of Children and Family Services, I was ready to protect myself.

This was the ultimate first step.

Over the next several weeks, Agent Fernandez scheduled various appointments for my son and me. Naiim and I entered counseling, alone and together, and Naiim underwent a series of medical and dental exams. I was evaluated by a team of psychiatrists and underwent the drug testing necessitated by the claims made against me. Naturally, all of our physical, mental, and emotional evaluations came back without any hiccups and my drug evaluation showed I had not consumed any drugs of any kind. Aeron's attempts to, once again, make me seem like a bad mother and person had failed. In many ways, I felt vindicated to be able to prove, for once, that everything he'd been saying about me was false. And after seeing how abusive Aeron had been to my son and me, including his most recent false claims, the Department of Children and Family Services took an even closer look at the case Jonah's mother had filed against him.

Aeron was in jeopardy of losing custody of Jonah and my restraining order against him had the potential to be the nail in the proverbial coffin. Even though I hadn't fought his petition for a restraining order against me years before, Aeron was hell-bent against letting me protect myself against him in a court of law. He enlisted one of his mother's best friends, an attorney he used to do most of his dirty work. What I hadn't foreseen, when filing the restraining order at the request of Agent Fernandez, was the legal fight Aeron would demand and the thousands of dollars it would cost me—money I didn't have. Even in my attempts to finally be free from Aeron, I stood to lose what little I had left.

Whether I wanted to go to court or not, I had to. The Department of Children and Family Services demanded I seek protection against Aeron with no concern as to the mental stress, anguish, anxiety, and financial burden it would cost. So, on May 5, 2011, I engaged an attorney and prepared to fight for my life. While the DCFS case against me dwindled, I appeared in a Los Angeles County court every two weeks as Aeron made sure my attempt to protect my son and myself against him dragged on. On every hearing date, I made my way to the courthouse, over an hour away from my apartment, sometimes accompanied by my attorney, sometimes not. I never even saw the inside of the courtroom as the attorneys met with the judge in his chambers, admitting evidence, only to have the case continued. And Aeron always came to the courthouse with a group of intimidators, including his mother. There were always at least four of them against me as I sat alone outside the courtroom, my stomach swirling and my heart racing.

There always seemed to be a reason for a continuance. Aeron always found a way to spin the truth in his favor and make me look like the psychopath, even though I was the one with the nearly endless paper trail of all he'd put me through.

I was under an exorbitant amount of stress and it was mostly evident in my massive weight loss. Nothing in my closet fit me anymore. Even my panties were too loose and I had to pin them to make them fit. I was sick and unable to bear the sight or smell of food. Every morning that I had to take the long drive to the courthouse, I vomited. The stress was just too much for me. All I wanted was to be free and to know that Aeron could be forced to stay away from me. All *he* wanted was to have full access to me and to keep Jonah's mother from having another piece of evidence that would help her regain custody of her son.

We were in court the entire month of May and into June, and the fact that I had to fight so hard and long to be protected against a man who had been physically abusing me for the past five years, when that abuse had been documented in police and injury reports, baffled me. I wondered what this process must be like for women with no resources and no documentation. I wondered about those women who, like me, had no family to support them and no one to protect them from monsters like Aeron. It made sense to me, all of a sudden, how so many women wind up dead at the hands of their abusers and why so many abusers meet the same fate at the hands of their victims. Aeron, his family, friends, and his attorney painted me as the aggressor and he as the victim, and the court seemed incapable of seeing Aeron's lies for what they were.

I was being blamed for being abused.

As mid-June approached, the Department of Children and Family Services closed their case against me and I was relieved to be finished with them. Around the same time, Aeron's case with DCFS was also closed and Agent Fernandez exited my life. One weight had been lifted from me but still a huge load remained. I was due back in court in about a week to continue my fight against Aeron and I was dreading it. It was difficult to know whether to keep going or cut my losses at that point. I'd invested over $10,000 and countless hours building my case with my attorney. The biggest part of me wanted to give up but it was overpowered by my need to win the order of protection. As horrible as I felt, as sick as the process was making me, I didn't know how to walk away—I didn't know if I should. As much as I wanted to quit, I was looking to be justified. I wanted to be protected! So, I geared up for another week of stress and anxiety as I prepared my documents for court.

CHAPTER SEVENTEEN

Same Tune

T here weren't many people in whom I could confide as I went through this latest ordeal with Aeron. I could always talk to Deneen, and she did her very best to support me from far away, but there was only so much she could do from Alabama. I spoke to her most every day, and on the days I was due in court, she stayed on the phone with me from the time I woke up until I arrived at the courthouse, then while I drove home. But, in between those phone calls, I felt alone. I was ashamed to tell anyone else that I'd let things with Aeron get this far. Everyone I knew had either warned me about him before or just after we began dating. Many of my friends gave up on me and on helping me to get away from Aeron after I continued to go back to him and defend him for so many years. I couldn't explain to any of them that I had let him back into my life after the move and all that decision had cost me.

Still, in the midst of all the chaos, I struggled to keep some sort of social life, to see friends when they were in town, and to laugh every once in a while—no matter how fake that laugh had to be. I stayed in contact with Shad's assistant, Ant, over the years, after being introduced to him while visiting Shad back in 2008. Shad and

I tried to keep in touch after I got back with Aeron in 2009, but life took us in different directions and our conversations became few and far between.

We managed to reunite in the summer of 2010 but were not as close as we used to be. Still, we kept in touch and saw one another most times he visited Los Angeles. Mainly, those visits were solemn, as I found it hard to engage, feeling far removed from the life I used to have and the woman I used to be. Shad often commented on my extreme weight loss and change in mood and all I could say was that I was going through something. I was too embarrassed to admit he was right when he told me how stupid I was to get back with Aeron, back in 2009. I was keeping all this pain, guilt, and shame buried deep inside and felt I was losing my mind more with every intimidating trip to the courthouse. I was about to break when, one day that June, I received a text from Ant that would change my life and turn everything around.

Ant and I had been text-messaging that night when he mentioned he was with Wayne and a few other friends we had in common. My heart swooned and my eyes watered as I realized just how awful my life had been since I walked away from Wayne nearly three years before.

I miss him so much, I texted back. *That man is the love of my life and I should have never let him go.*

I'm here with him, he wrote, *and I showed him your text messages. He smiled real big. Said to call him.*

Ant gave me Wayne's phone number and I frantically dialed. It rang. I held my breath. It rang some more. I shivered. The call went to voicemail. With my hands shaking, I proceeded to text him. *Hey, babe. It's Karrine.*

Babe! he replied.

Hi! I miss you, I typed as I began to cry.

I need to see you when I get to LA.

Of course! Just let me know when. Baby, I love you and I miss you so much.

Love you, too. Miss you. See you soon.

Days later, I got the call. I got out of bed and did my best to pull myself together, self-conscious of my thinning hair and gaunt body. I put on my makeup and pulled together an outfit, ran to my car, and sped out of the garage and into the darkness. I was nervous. I felt like I was going to be sick. My whole world was about to change and seeing him again was nearly too much to bear.

I pulled up to the studio and texted him, *I'm here.*

Someone's coming, he replied.

Seconds later, a burly security guard came out to greet me, confirm my identity, and open the gate. I drove into the parking lot, parked, took a deep breath, and headed in to find my love. I walked into the recording studio shortly after 3 AM and saw him for the first time in almost three years. He sat at the soundboard, his back to me, listening to songs he'd created for his upcoming album, *Tha Carter IV*. He bobbed his head and tapped his feet. His dreadlocks hung much longer than they had nearly three years before and were now touching the middle of his back. They were tied with a rubber band and adorned with a fitted baseball cap. I was almost afraid for him to turn around. I lost my nerve and my breath.

I'd been through so much since I'd seen him last. I'd been ruined. I'd lost everything and forgotten who I was. I had been used and abused, and left for dead. I put up with shit from someone I would have never stayed with if I would have just stayed with Wayne through all *his* bullshit, all the disappointment that came with *him*. The devil I knew was better than the devil I didn't. Fuck! What if I wasn't good enough for him anymore? What if he took one look at me and saw how broken I was and wanted nothing to do with the shell I'd become? It took everything I had not to cry right then and there. I felt weak, my heart raced. All I wanted to do was fall into his arms and weep.

Then Wayne looked forward and saw my reflection in the glass that separated the studio from the recording booth. He turned around in his swivel chair, rose to his feet, and opened his arms. It all seemed to happen in slow-motion, like a dream sequence. In fact, I guess it was. It was the dream I'd been dreaming for the past three years. Now, here it was—here he was—and my nightmares were over. He had no idea the journey I had without him. He had no idea how bad it had all gotten, how much I'd lost, and how much had been taken from me. I fell into him and held him tightly, like it was the end of the world.

And I was saved.

There was so much I wanted to say, so much I needed to tell him. I wanted to cry. Bawl. I wanted to fall to the floor and kiss his fucking feet! I was overwhelmed but I kept it all together, looking at the handful of people in the room, afraid to be vulnerable in front of them.

"Hey, babe! How have you been?" he asked as he embraced me.

Ugh. I wanted to just blurt it all out. I wanted to tell him I'd been doing horribly, that I married a monster and ruined my life, that I was devastated by the secret he kept from me all those years ago and shattered by my decision to leave, but all that came out was, "I'm good, babe," as I squeezed his muscular frame and inhaled his scent, burying my nose in his neck among his dreads. Trying my hardest to keep cool, I peeled myself away from him and took a seat on a nearby sofa. He sat back in the swivel chair and spun it around to face me.

"You look good, babe," he assured me, even though I didn't. Not really. Not to me. I just wasn't at my best with all the weight loss and my thinning hair slicked back in a ponytail, my nails undone, and my face tired. But it was dark in the studio and he hadn't seen me in years.

"Thanks. You, too. I'm so happy to see you."

"I'm happy to see you, too, babe. For real."

I was greeted warmly and hugged by members of Wayne's crew and I felt at home—more at home than I'd felt in a long time. The loud music, the weed smoke, the laughter. I was surrounded by people I knew and I was safe. Comfortable. Wayne was more jovial than I remembered him. He was lively and cracking jokes. He held court in the studio, telling stories and revealing the secret menu items at fast-food restaurants like the McGang Bang at McDonald's. We all laughed, holding our stomachs at times and keeling over.

He was beautiful.

He was perfect.

Wayne doted on me, as he always had in the past, making sure I had everything I needed while at the studio with him. We talked a bit; he asked about my son and I asked about his four children—he'd fathered two more by two more women since I last saw him. We talked about the old days, things we'd done, places we'd been, and he reminded me of who I was. I'd become so accustomed to being broken down and devoid of spirit that it was hard for me to remember the old me, the lively me who awoke with a smile every morning. I was happy when I was with Wayne and miserable without him.

With joy in my heart and a smile of contentment upon my face, I looked around that dark, smoky studio and realized something. I wasn't normal. Nor was anyone there, that night. And nothing about my life had ever been ordinary, common, average, or regular. I'd been chasing something that was never meant for me, and on that night, I decided I wouldn't chase it anymore. It was the idea that I had to be normal, the notion that being different was wrong, that had driven me into a horrible marriage, a painful divorce, and now a disturbing, drawn-out court case. But as I looked around the studio and the people in it, I realized that I had access to something so many "normal" people wish they had—these non-normal, extraordinary moments of pure insanity, of laughter, inside a dark room with people who didn't judge, who didn't care, who were just there for the love of it. I wasn't normal and I could never *have* normal and that had to be okay with me.

It was nearly 7 AM when we all oozed out of the recording studio. I was exhausted but full of life and looking forward to spending some quiet time alone with Wayne. He hopped into a chauffeured Cadillac SUV and I followed behind in my Mercedes. The streets were empty and the sun shone a yellowish-orange. It was a beautiful morning. As I followed behind Wayne's car to the Montage Hotel in Beverly Hills, I practiced what I would say when we were finally alone for the first time in so long.

"Wayne, that day on the bus, I was upset because . . ."

No. I didn't think that was a good starting point.

"Babe, I love you so much and I'm so sorry for . . ."

Fuck! That was too sappy. He'd never respond to that.

"Take me with you. Wherever you're going, just fucking take me with you!"

Yeah, no.

Upon our arrival, we entered through the backside of the building. We walked through the bowels of the hotel and into the service elevator, which took us to the top floor. Without saying much, I hopped into the shower as he ordered a cup of coffee and popped in a CD of his new music for *Tha Carter IV*. I wrapped myself in a robe and settled onto the sofa, beside him.

"My back hurts, babe," he announced, softly, while reaching for a spot between his shoulder blades.

I rushed to soothe him. I rose from my seat and walked into the bathroom to fetch a bottle of lotion. Returning, I slid between him and the sofa and proceeded to rub his back and shoulders. I ran my fingers over his tattoos, tracing them, following them like a trail back home. I found my way back to his gunshot scar, and as I always had, I lowered my lips, kissed it, and said a silent prayer, thanking God for saving his life and bringing him back to me.

I wanted to tell him everything. I wanted to tell him how sorry I was for walking away from him and all the shit I'd gone through because of it. I wanted to tell him why I left. I wanted him to know how I cried when he went to prison and when he was released. I wanted to say so much but I couldn't. I wouldn't burden him or us with the past. Wayne and I had been given a second chance and I was determined to never let him go or not push him away again. So instead, I pulled his body into mine, I took him into me, and made love to him all morning long.

CHAPTER EIGHTEEN

It Was All So Ridiculous

wo days after being reunited with Wayne, I was scheduled to be in court with Aeron to continue fighting for a restraining order against him. This was our fourth or fifth appearance in court and every time we went, he would show up with his attorney, his mother, other family members and friends, or even his mother's next-door neighbor, for Christ's sake. As for me, over the past months, I'd just show up all alone, gaunt and feeble, clutching my papers, sitting in a corner by myself, looking at the floor, and waiting to be called. They had been like a pack of wolves and I was alone with no support, just trying to get this man out of my life for good.

After being with Wayne, however, I no longer felt alone or outnumbered. I was empowered by him and infected with his swagger. Before, I'd vomit every morning before going to court, my stomach nervous and unsettled. But, on this morning, I awoke and felt nothing. I couldn't have given less of a shit about Aeron or his band of intimidators. They were all a bunch of nobodies and has-beens and Wayne had reminded me that I was a star, a light, and I deserved to shine again. I was ready to take back what my relationship with Aeron had taken from me. I was back with Wayne and divorced from Aeron; I was in the perfect position to start over, and going back and forth to court, holding on and contributing to the negative energy that had held me captive for so long was only doing me a disservice. I could see that, now. So, I walked into the courthouse that morning with just one agenda—dropping my case.

For the first time in years, I could eat again. After being with Wayne, I was suddenly hungry. I was happy. Beaming. I had confidence again and I now knew who I was and what I was worth. I dropped my request for the restraining order and Aeron dropped his request to renew the original restraining order he imposed before we were married. I walked out of that courtroom, head held high, with a big, bright smile on my face, my ex-husband trailing behind.

"Maybe we can go to a movie or something this weekend," he suggested.

"Sure!" I replied. I kissed and hugged his mother and everyone else he had with him that day.

"I love you, Karrine," Mona insisted. "I wish you guys didn't have to put each other through all this. You should bring Naiim by the house to play with the other grandkids sometime next week!"

"Sure!" I replied, before waving good-bye to my past, taking the long walk back to my car, and driving into my future. I was smiling so hard, my face hurt. I was just so happy. I drove away from that courthouse, determined to never see it again. And I didn't call Aeron, or visit my ex-mother-in-law.

I just fucking left.

I never told Wayne what he did for me or about my battles with my ex-husband. He never knew about my inability to eat or the physical changes I'd gone through from the stress and pressure of being in such a tormenting relationship. The vomiting, the nerves, my thinning hair and yellowing nails, the weight loss, the loss of all my confidence and self-worth—he never knew about it. He never heard about the beatings, the choking—not since he hung up on me the night of my birthday when I tried to confide in him about the first time Aeron abused me. His pride would never have allowed him to allow me to tell him about any other man in my life. I learned on that night, back in 2007, that Wayne didn't want to know everything—or anything at all, except that I loved him. But I often wanted to tell him how *his* power empowered me and gave me everything I needed to leave the worst relationship of my life, how by just being in my life again, he'd given me something no one else could. I'd left a piece of myself with him on that bus back in 2008 and, unbeknownst to him, he'd carried it with him during our years apart. Now, I had it back. He'd given me back a piece of myself and completed me.

Still, after all of that, after finally getting back to the place I belonged and to the man I loved, and after making my escape from a horrific life with Aeron, Aeron and I were not over. With no restraining orders with which to contend, Aeron began coming back around and courting me. He'd oftentimes show up with a bouquet of my favorite flowers, red roses and star lilies, and a box of chocolates or something else delectably sweet. He was pouring it on thick and talking about getting back together, remarried even, but I wasn't interested—not in a romantic relationship with him and certainly not in remarrying him.

I was invigorated, falling back into the skin of the person I used to be. I was stronger and more resilient. I was beautiful again and feeling better than I had since I left Wayne that day on the tour bus. I had pep in my step, a sway in my hair, and a gleam of light in my eye. I was coming alive again, and even though there was nothing to stop Aeron from popping up at my doorstep, there was a wall keeping him from lunging back into my heart and mind. I was back with Wayne and nothing and no one could bring me down. Long gone was the sorry sap looking for normalcy or to be secured by a man, family, and the look of perfection.

For the first time in four years, I wouldn't be going back to Aeron.

However, I felt bad for our children, these two innocent boys, brothers, who were being torn apart by abuse and divorce. Mostly,

I felt sorry for Jonah. I felt bad that he didn't have sameness and a place to call home. There was very little stability in his life and he never knew where he would be from one day to the next or who would be picking him up from school. Even though everyone surrounding him were family and friends, children thrive on stability and repetition, and it seemed extremely rare for him to ever have the same day twice.

As it happened, my new apartment was just one block away from CBS studios, where Aeron filmed the soap opera, and about eight minutes from the school Jonah attended. So, with Aeron not having a stable home, it was convenient for him to come by my place with Jonah during the week. His alternative was to drive out to his mother's house, over an hour away—two hours in traffic. As always, I was convenient for Aeron, but between my guilt about the children and Aeron's rambling ways, I didn't mind allowing him and Jonah to spend time or sleep at my place. It was nice to have the kids back together, again. I enjoyed being able to get Jonah ready for school, ironing his uniform and preparing his lunches. It felt good to be a mom to him again. Naiim, however, seemed to be annoyed with the whole situation. He hadn't fallen into the old routines he once had with Jonah. He was a bit older and a lot wiser and still harbored hurt over the pain Aeron caused him and me over the years.

And I couldn't blame him.

Though Naiim was cordial, he was never really into it and was simply tolerating having Aeron and Jonah back in our lives. As for me, I felt safe. Aeron was no longer a threat to me. Having Wayne back in my life was a serious boost and I was dating other people, as well. I was going out again, accepting invitations to parties, and taking trips with friends.

Then, I remarried.

In August 2011, I met a man who lived in my apartment complex. I'd seen him around often. He was an ugly man, dark-skinned and very short. His hair was dreadlocked and his island accent was very heavy. I could tell he was Jamaican and figured he was somehow related to Rohan Marley, son of Bob Marley. Rohan lived upstairs and he and I had a brief series of intimate encounters soon after I moved into the building eight months prior. Nothing more ever came of it, but Rohan and I remained cordial neighbors. After seeing him numerous times around the property and in the parking garage, often driving Rohan's cars, the mysterious Jamaican finally spoke and we were introduced. His name was Nigel and he was Rohan's cousin, temporarily in the United States on a work visa.

There was something endearing and indigenous about Nigel. He reminded me of home. Born and raised in the Virgin Islands, I was very accustomed to his way of speech and his way of life, his cooking, and I related to the memories he had of growing up in Jamaica. We connected on these points and I thought he was exactly what I needed in my life, at the time. I needed someone to keep Aeron away, first and foremost. He was a watchdog of sorts. Plus, Nigel would provide balance. I could have late studio nights and days of intimate private time with Wayne and then this regular island life at home when I wasn't with the love of my life. Essentially, I created a scenario in my head, the perfect arrangement and its benefits to me. Nigel would be my houseboy—the kind of man I thought Aeron was when he and I first started dating back in 2007. I could have Nigel at the apartment to keep the home fires burning while I ran around town living my life, regaining my independence, confidence, and the inspiration to get back to work.

While I am obviously a woman and possess many traditional feminine qualities, much of my personality and many of my traits can be described as traditionally masculine. There were times during my relationship and marriage to Aeron when I was content to be the housewife, cooking and cleaning for my family. But, unlike most housewives, I was doing all of that *and* making all the money *and* paying all the bills. Initially, with Aeron, what I wanted and thought I was getting was a man who would support my endeavors at home while I strengthened my career and built my fortune. I didn't mind paying all the bills, as long as my ability to work and live the life I wanted was not obstructed. I didn't want a rival and I certainly didn't want an oppressor.

Well, that plan blew up in my face.

This time, I would choose a man who had nothing to lose and everything to gain by supporting me. I imagined he'd cook and clean and make sure the car got washed. He would take care of the tedious responsibilities of home life while I worked on my appearance, my social life, and regaining my footing in publishing. It had been two years since my publisher dropped me, and I desperately needed a way back into the industry. In return for all his hard work and dedication to my success, he'd be well taken care of and married to me and eventually, if all went well, he could get his American citizenship. Plus, he would help me project a picture of normalcy to the public while I ran around being as un-normal as fucking possible. Though I no longer wanted the same things I sought in past relationships, I knew the public needed to see me being more like them, if only for a moment. Nigel would provide the perfect public smoke screen while I focused on my relationship with Wayne, privately.

I told Nigel the whole thing wouldn't last more than two years, though he always laughed when I said it. I told him I had a plan but didn't divulge its details. Nigel had no idea what he was getting himself into, but he was in a desperate situation. Rohan made it possible for him to obtain the work visa by claiming to hire Nigel, and though Nigel did work for him as a gofer, he wasn't paid well. I was offering Nigel everything he needed as long as he gave me everything I needed. The plan was perfect and he went along with it, easily, not knowing all the details.

Five weeks after meeting Nigel, in September 2011, he and I were married. The ceremony was held in the same chapel where Aeron and I were wed, and the managers of the establishment gave me a 10 percent discount for being a repeat customer. Seriously. This time, I bought a dress—a cocktail-length lace number by Betsey Johnson. I also bought outfits for Nigel and Naiim and enlisted one bridesmaid, who bought me the perfect bouquet of roses and star lilies. I knew this was more of a business agreement than it was a marriage, but I wanted to have a little fun with the wedding and make it somewhat different from the one I had with Aeron. One thing was for sure, I wouldn't be getting choked and spit upon once I got home.

During the ceremony, when the officiant read the section of vows that spoke of faithfulness, I stalled while repeating them. I smirked. I wanted to bust out in a fit of laughter because Nigel and I both knew this marriage was never going to be about faithfulness. Nigel lowered his chin, staring up at me as I sputtered the words, "I promise to be faithful." The truth was, even if I was in love with this man and had every intention of having a traditional, monogamous marriage with him, there was no way I would have been able to. In addition to his physical unattractiveness, Nigel was not a very smart man. Though he had more than his share of vocational knowledge, he lacked book smarts and I found myself having to correct him often as he used words that simply did not exist. All in all, Nigel was not a catch and was certainly no one to whom I'd consider being faithful! So, I repeated the faithfulness vow and all the other erroneous vows with a roll of my eyes and a smirk on my face.

It was all so ridiculous.

After the ceremony, I skipped out of the chapel, bouquet in hand, happy to have completed the first steps of my plan to regain my life. I was married to a man I didn't love but who wouldn't beat me. All he had to do was take care of me and in a couple years, he could have his citizenship. We passed by a barbershop just two doors down from the chapel, Nigel trailing behind me, followed by Naiim and my lone bridesmaid. Outside the shop there were three barbers sitting there, on a break. One of the barbers wore long, neat dreadlocks and seemed to be of island descent.

He extended his hand to Nigel. "You guys just got married?" the stranger asked.

"Yeah, man!" Nigel replied, happily.

"Congratulations!"

"Thank you. Thank you."

The two men shared a congratulatory fist bump.

It was all so ridiculous.

Nigel came into the arrangement knowing I had a plan and knowing all about my relationship with Wayne. During those first five weeks before we were wed, I saw Wayne quite often and never felt the need to hide the relationship from Nigel or anyone else. I was back where I belonged and anyone wanting to be in my life would either have to accept my relationship with Wayne or be shown the door.

I was never going to leave him again.

Days later, I received a phone call from Aeron. "I heard you got married," he said in his deep, growling voice.

I was stunned. "How'd you hear that? I haven't told anyone."

"I got a call from my barber."

"Oh."

CHAPTER NINETEEN

And Again

Upon hearing of my recent nuptials, Aeron stayed away and I was happy about that. I was determined to have my relationships by *my* rules and to never again be and feel as helpless and broken as I was in my first marriage. I assured Nigel there would be no second chances for him in our arrangement. To put it plainly, I was done taking people's shit. Other than Wayne, a man would either do what I said or be shown the door. I was no longer interested in being under anyone's tyrannical rule. I was growing stronger by the day, and while I knew I would have a long road back to recovery, I also knew I had to start somewhere. I had to go into my new relationships with my eyes wide open and my guard up. Under no circumstances was I to fall in love with the men I would meet or the ideals they would try to sell me. I was struggling to regain my footing and I was in no way interested in having a man come into my life, distracting me from the pressing matters at hand.

I was in charge and I was focused.

However, I was still trying to dig myself out of a financial hole and my career had long stalled, even though my fourth book, *Satis-Faction: Erotic Fantasies for the Advanced and Adventurous Couple*, had just been published. There were no new deals in sight and I wasn't even sure of the direction in which I wanted my career to go. I knew I wanted to create something bigger, something I cared about and not just what publishers or readers wanted from me. I wanted to do something meaningful but struggled with what that would be. I straddled the fence between wanting to reveal what my life was really like and continuing to publicly perpetuate the kind of life the public thought I was living. I wanted to show the world who I really was and what my home life was really like, including the adoration of a husband who was so grateful to be married to me, he did everything I asked, all day, every day. He was subservient and I loved it. He did most of the cooking and cleaning and chauffeured me around. Every morning and evening after my showers, I'd lay naked on the bed while he massaged my entire body with lotions and oils. Nigel was devoted to his new position but, apparently, my husband didn't take me seriously when I told him what I expected of him.

Just a little over one month after we were wed, my arrangement with Nigel was already over. The only stipulations I'd given him were that he was to do whatever I told him and under no circumstances was he to ever break my trust. Just days after our wedding, he flew to Jamaica to spend a month with his son—a flight for which I paid. While he was there, I sent him money for food and bills since the man hadn't a dollar to his name. I upheld my part of the deal and took care of Nigel *and* his son, expecting him to remain honest. Still, my intuition told me he wasn't, though it wouldn't be until Nigel returned home in November that I would catch him in a series of lies.

Just a few days after his return, I'd put Nigel to work rebuilding the master bedroom closet. My apartment was small and my bedroom seemed to be built for just one person, so while Nigel was away, I'd measured and planned how to maximize the closet for us both. Then, with the plans I made, we visited IKEA and The Home Depot for supplies. Nigel was a hardworking man who had all sorts of skills. He could rebuild car engines and had worked in construction back in Jamaica. He looked forward to the task of rebuilding the closet and I was happy to help however I could.

But, while Nigel worked, I noticed he was continually receiving text messages and responding to them. Every minute or two, his phone would chime and he would promptly return the text before returning to his work in the closet. My suspicions and sixth sense couldn't take it anymore. I needed to know what and who was in that phone.

"I'll be right back," I said as I picked up his phone. "I'm going to the bathroom with your phone and I think you know why."

Nigel looked up at me from the floor of the closet, stunned and afraid. "Okay," he said nervously. I walked calmly into the bathroom and locked the door behind me. Seconds later, Nigel stood on the other side of the door. "Babe," he said. "Babe!"

I stood there silently as I rummaged through his phone. As I suspected, the recent rash of text messages he'd received were from a woman he was with while in Jamaica. I fumed. Upon further snooping, I found a slew of text messages from over twenty women all over the world, all of them inappropriate. Then, I found the most disturbing set of messages of them all. While away, he had been busy chatting with and wooing a woman who lived next door to Rohan, trying to persuade her to join him on the island. After skimming through his phone further, I found messages between them in which he was trying to convince her to be with him here in the United States and evidence of his visiting her apartment just two days after his return home. As irritated as I was to be footing the bill for this loser only for him to do the one thing I'd asked him not to, I was more tickled by the fact that someone so broke, so black, so short, so ugly, and so stupid could have over twenty women on his phone at one time.

I was fucking floored!

I warned my husband before we were married that there would be no second chances for him. I warned him that if he broke my trust, if I found him to be a liar, a sneak, a cheat, or a fraud, that it would be the end of our little arrangement.

I said it and I meant it.

It was just days before Thanksgiving when I found out about my husband's trysts and infidelities, so immediately upon my discovery, I demanded Nigel pack his shit and leave. He cried like a baby and even got on his knees and begged for my forgiveness. He must've pleaded, even as he packed, for two hours, but I didn't care. I tried to deliver him back to Rohan and even Rohan's brother, Chris, who also lived in the complex, but they refused him. Nobody wanted Nigel. So, there I was, stuck with a husband I didn't want, who had nowhere else to go at a time of the year when everyone he knew was out of town with their families. Begrudgingly, I let him stay with me through the holiday season and into the New Year.

Nigel and I celebrated the holidays as a fake family and continued about our daily lives as if everything wasn't completely ruined. He continued taking care of the household chores while I continued supporting him. He overcompensated for his mistakes and tried too hard to make our arrangement into a real relationship. He knew he was on thin ice and, with his citizenship hanging in the balance, he was trying everything he knew to be the perfect husband and houseboy, but it was too late.

Naturally, I continued to see Wayne. He always had a special ringtone in my phone, which rang even if my ringer was turned off. It was always one of his songs and I made sure the volume of the ringtone was at its highest, accompanied by vibration. There was no way I would miss any of his calls or text messages. He had complete and total access to me any and every time of the day and night. The calls and texts would come at random times, because of the somewhat random hours of his professional and personal schedule. I'd leave the house early in the morning to see Wayne and tell Nigel I was headed to a breakfast meeting, or go over to Wayne's hotel in the middle of the afternoon, claiming to be running errands. I just didn't feel the need to explain to Nigel where I was going, when I'd be back, and with whom I was spending my time. Our marriage was a sham of an arrangement and he had already proven he could not be trusted. I was just biding my time until I got rid of him.

I felt more in charge of my life than I'd felt in years, and the truth of the matter was that I took on a persona very reminiscent of Aeron's. I did what I wanted when I wanted with no conscience or worries of repercussions. I was free of the chains that had bound me for so long and there was nothing that could keep me from my happiness. I was determined to have what and who I wanted, when I wanted. I felt as if I had earned the right to run my life and do whatever I pleased, no matter what.

After the holiday season, I stuck to my guns and let Nigel know he was still expected to move out. His cousins were back from their vacations abroad, but still neither Rohan nor his brother, Chris, wanted anything to do with Nigel. So, in January, he packed up and went to live with a friend he knew from Jamaica who lived deep on the outskirts of the San Fernando Valley, about fifty-five minutes away from me.

I was ecstatic.

It didn't take long after cutting ties with Nigel to realize that my newly rediscovered ability to run my life, and the power that came from that feeling, had overtaken my good sense and judgment when it came to my plan for marriage. I'd been drunk with it, still trying to prove something. I felt the need to show that my divorce from Aeron wasn't my fault, that I was lovable and capable of getting someone else to marry me despite Aeron's insistence I never would. Even though I was resigned to the fact that I would never *be* normal, I still, even now, wanted to at least *appear* normal. But I shook that notion almost immediately after it came.

I didn't need a marriage to validate me, publicly or otherwise.

Since putting Nigel out of the apartment, he found it difficult to stay away. He had become so accustomed to being home with me and doing things for me, it seemed as if he didn't know who he was or what to do without me. I understood that feeling. Still, he soon grew into a needy nuisance. He begged to come by at least once a week, sometimes two, to watch our favorite television shows. He wanted to keep in touch with Naiim who, at this point, didn't care who came and went out of our lives. He was over it, just as I was.

I was trying to wean Nigel from my bosom and began revoking his visitation privileges, little by little, until I'd had enough and cut him off altogether. He needed to begin his own routines and traditions and to break away from the ones we'd formed during his stay with me. And I needed to stop giving him pity sex. I had to put an end to everything.

So, in March 2012, after a few weeks apart, I called Nigel over and, jovially, he met me at my apartment with hope in his eyes. We sat on the sofa, watching our shows, eating dinner, then dessert, drinking wine, and being cordial. But I was withdrawn. I waited until our programs were over before reaching underneath one of the sofa's cushions, pulling out a folder, and handing it to him.

"What's this?" he asked, with trepidation.

"I've had divorce papers drawn up. All you have to do is sign them," I cautiously replied.

As Nigel thumbed through the paperwork, his energy changed. He began to panic. Everything was coming to an end for him. I understood that feeling, too.

He jumped up from the sofa. "I'm not signing this," he insisted.

"That's a joint dissolution. You don't have to sign it, but if we both sign those papers, it'll be over faster and easier. If you don't sign it, I can always do it the other way, which means that I can file on my own, have you served, and no matter what you do, we'll still be divorced in six months."

Nigel's eyes began to dart as he paced the apartment wildly. He began muttering and tripping over his words. "I'm not signing anything. I need to have an attorney look over this," he insisted as a way to stall the inevitable.

"Attorney? You don't even have a car and you're talking to me about attorneys? Look, this is a standard form. Look at it! It's easy to comprehend. Read it and just sign it!"

But Nigel wouldn't go away that easily.

He was terrified of losing me completely, knowing his chance of American citizenship was slipping away. But whether we were married or not, I no longer had any intention of helping him gain citizenship. And I had no intention of establishing a life together. He had already shown himself to be untrustworthy and I was finished. The marriage alone wouldn't guarantee him a green card. The marriage would have to be entered into in good faith, and I would have to pay thousands of dollars, fill out mountains of paperwork, and subject myself to government protocol. He was no longer worth it.

We argued for the next two hours as Nigel refused to sign the papers and then refused to leave the apartment. He begged me to change my mind and pleaded with me to just sit and talk everything through. He apologized for his mistakes and promised to do better, but I wasn't interested in any of that. Eventually, I had to pretend to call the police to get Nigel to leave, without signing the joint dissolution. Several weeks later, I filed another set of divorce papers and had Nigel served.

He dragged out the proceedings, and it took over a year for our divorce to become final.

In the meantime, Aeron's radar sent off a signal, letting him know I was free.

It had been six months since Nigel and I married, and during that time, Aeron waited in the wings, keeping in contact via email and sporadic phone calls. Soon after Nigel's departure, the calls and emails became more frequent. It was as if he knew I was alone. When I confirmed that Nigel was gone for good, Aeron expected to pop back into my life and take what he felt was his rightful place by my side. He began frequenting my apartment with Jonah, again. It was ironic, but the moment I stopped needing to be part of a family, realizing that Naiim and I were family enough, Aeron made himself and Jonah more available to us than he had in prior years, wanting to become members of *our* family.

But it was too late.

Though I enjoyed their company and I loved being there for Jonah, my heart had moved on. Aeron struggled as he tried to draw me back into his world. He kept looking for signs that I was falling back under his spell but the signs never came. I didn't need him to love or validate me anymore. But what I *did* need was financial assistance.

There were parts of my life I could never explain to Wayne, Shad, Ant, or anyone else. If I told them I'd lost everything, I'd have to answer the questions that would follow. Questions about Aeron and Nigel, questions about why I hadn't acquired another book deal since being released from my last contract in 2010 and what I'd been doing with my life and money over the past several years. I couldn't stand the possibility of having to explain the mess my life had become and the bad decisions I made along the way, so I kept my troubles to myself. I never divulged my financial woes to them, just as I never divulged all I'd gone through with Aeron over the years. Therefore, I could never ask for financial help from friends who had the ability to help me.

I couldn't bear the shame.

Soon, it was summer, and even though I was completely over Aeron, I was still suffering from the decision I made to let him into my life back in 2007. I returned my Range Rover and my Mercedes Benz E-Class, all to the detriment of my credit, and purchased a used Mercedes C-Class soon after moving into the new apartment. I was struggling to pay my $3,000 rent and my car note, as well as for everyday essentials like groceries and utilities. I lost most everything I'd worked so hard to earn and now I needed help to maintain the few things I had left.

Every little bit helped.

My friend Bruce had been doing a good job of assisting me over the past couple of years. He and I met way back in 2006 and became fast friends. We never dated but shared intimacies; I saw him as just a friend as he was never my type. So, when he entered into a relationship and got engaged in 2007, I was happy for him and hoped he would forget all about our trysts and focus on being just friends.

And he did—until I needed money.

As with most of my friends, Bruce was accustomed to me having my own everything. I had been self-sufficient for the majority of the time we'd known one another, making it easy for me to shrug off his advances. When my circumstances changed and I began needing more and more help, Bruce used the opportunity to make me earn the money I needed. Disgustingly, he turned our relationship from platonic to sex-for-hire, and I felt like I had no choice but to let him. I was now living mostly off of my bi-yearly residual checks, and even though I was no longer shelling out $20,000 a month in bills, my living expenses, coupled with previous debts related to my marriage to Aeron, were still too much for me to handle. I wasn't sinking as quickly as I was before, but I was sinking nonetheless.

By the time I left my home and moved into the apartment in the city, Bruce was sporadically chipping in to help me pay for my basic day-to-day needs between residual checks. As time went on and more of his money was spent, he began asking for favors like foot rubs or manicures. Over time, the tasks became more demeaning and, after a while, wound up being purely sexual. There wasn't a time after mid-2011 that Bruce gave me money before or without some sort of sexual favor. By the time I wiggled myself free from my legal woes with Aeron, I had dug an even deeper hole with Bruce. Still, he spoke of our arrangement as if it were some sort of functioning relationship. He often mentioned how safe he felt with me and how close we had grown over the years. It was as if we were having two different relationships—because we were. Bruce was happy to have me in his grip and I was praying to God for a way out.

CHAPTER TWENTY

The Way Out

As my financial troubles mounted, Aeron did his best to help out around the apartment, paying for groceries and small bills while Bruce mostly took care of my rent during the leaner months. In just five years, I had managed to go from a completely self-sufficient woman with a thriving career to an out-of-work author depending on the men in my life to keep me afloat. More than that, I was depending on the two men I loathed the most to stay alive. Bruce had turned our friendship into a financial arrangement and Aeron hadn't changed in all the years I'd known him. He was still throwing tantrums and trying to affect me with the same games like disappearing for days or a week at a time. The only difference was that, this time, I didn't go chasing after him. When he got jealous about my dealings with Wayne or my ongoing friendship with Shad, he would take off and stay gone, waiting for me to call or text. I wouldn't, and after a week of no contact, he'd return. His old tricks no longer garnered any fanfare or uproar from me. There was no chasing or calling or driving around in the middle of the night searching for him.

Those days were over.

I was spending most of my time with Wayne and dabbling in dating others. I was single and free of emotional bondage for the first time in years and enjoying it. But I still had no idea what my next professional move would be. I didn't know what my readers wanted from me and I wasn't able to give publishers the smut they wanted. I'd been through so much since the publication of *Confessions of a Video Vixen*, and my life was vastly different. Publishers may have thought I was living some sort of high life, running around with one celebrity and the next, but that was all part of the persona, a persona that had taken on a life of its own. I couldn't give them a book about a life I wasn't living. I couldn't give them a book about anything! I was in some sort of purgatory between wellness and sickness, teetering between utter failure and rekindled success. I kept pulling myself out of one ditch only to land in another. By September 2012, I was barely making it, running out of money and time.

And then the bottom fell out.

I needed both Aeron and Bruce to help me make ends meet while I taught myself the ins and outs of self-publishing. The industry had changed dramatically over the past seven years since my entree into it and I needed to educate myself on all the ways I could make books and money on my own, in the event no publisher would ever want to sign me again. So, I focused on researching the information I would need to be a successful self-publisher while also beginning to rebrand myself and my online presence, slowly chipping away at the harmful persona I created. I had a long-term plan. It took several years to dig this ditch and I needed time and financial help to dig my way out.

Aeron didn't have an issue with Bruce, but Bruce had an issue with my relationship with Aeron, unbeknownst to me. So, when Bruce shorted me $800 that month and I couldn't pay the rent, I didn't understand how he could just sit back and watch me get evicted. This is a man who loved to remind me what a true friend he was, even though all the money he handed me was now attached to sex. And even though he had millions of dollars in the bank, he insisted this was all he could do.

I didn't fight.

I had no fight left.

After turning in the keys to my apartment, Naiim and I squeezed into my car, filled with personal belongings, and checked into an extended-stay hotel in the suburb of Woodland Hills on September 11, 2012. I walked away from the apartment and from Aeron after seeing the monster inside him rear its head, once again. As he punched a hole in the pantry door, a switch was flipped and all of a sudden, I was just done with him. After all he'd done, after all the trouble, the beatings, the choking, the spitting, the allegations, and after all his efforts to end my life and livelihood, *that* was it.

A fist through the cabinet did it.

With the majority of my belongings in storage, Naiim and I settled into the hotel with a few suitcases of clothing and toiletries and a large tote filled with food. Our room couldn't have been more than 600 square feet, with one queen-size bed, a bathroom, a desk, chair, TV, small closet, and a kitchen, complete with pots, dishes, utensils, a full-size refrigerator, and stove top.

For the next two and a half months, my son and I would call this place home.

The irony was, my son and I lived in this same hotel before, way back in the year 2000, a time I wrote about in *Confessions of a Video Vixen*. I was homeless back then, too, before there were any books, any *Oprah* appearances, first-class book tours, and infamy. I was right back where I started. The significance of this wasn't lost on me. As painful as this time in my life was, I knew it was necessary. I knew it would be uncomfortable and I would have to go through the darkest of tunnels before seeing the light. I knew God had something for me and after all the mistakes I made, after all the lessons I refused to heed, I was ready for my punishment.

I couldn't run from it anymore.

We settled into the hotel with only enough money for a week's stay, and as much as I hated depending on Bruce and the turn our friendship had taken because of that dependence, he was the only person I had. But the idea of groveling and humbling myself to him after he purposely shorted me on the rent pained me. I was determined to make it without him as long as I could. There were just three weeks until my next residual check and with it I would be able to move into a new place and start over. So, I hunkered down and prepared for whatever lay ahead.

There was no way to deny I did this to myself.

As I sat on the bed in that tiny hotel room, watching my son sink into the recliner with his laptop, a wave of guilt came over me.

I did it to him, too.

In my mind, I reviewed all that happened over the past five years and wondered where it all started, where it all went wrong. It would have been easy to take it back to when I was a child. I could have blamed it all on the bloody beatings my mother gave me, on the fact that she never hugged me or told me she loved me except once, at the urging of a friend. I could have blamed it on my absentee father who, even though he tried to remain in my life when I was a child, hadn't succeeded. Though he did everything he could for me after I was sent to live with him after I threatened to kill my abusive mother, he had never been a nurturer. I could have blamed my bad decisions on the man who kidnapped and raped me repeatedly for three days when I was thirteen years old. I could have blamed them on the other man who kidnapped me and held me at gunpoint when I was sixteen, ordering me to have sex with him before the gun jammed and I fled.

My list of childhood and adolescent atrocities goes on and on, and sure, I could have blamed it on all the horrible things that happened to me in my formative years when I should have been learning how to become a virtuous woman, but instead was taught about abuse, fear, neglect, and insurmountable pain. Every adult in my life had dumped their shit on me since I was born and I could easily have blamed my current circumstances all on them.

But I didn't.

The event that triggered a domino effect of ill-fated choices and unfortunate events was that kiss. It was the day I let Aeron close enough to touch me. It had taken five years for me to break free from his clutches and still I was under his curse. I knew then that I would never see or speak to Aeron again, just as I knew I would have to work harder than I'd ever worked to get back to where I'd been before I let him into my life. And the work would start there, in that room, on that day.

I vowed to keep my focus and find the inspiration to write again. I immersed myself in ideas and research. I was feeling more motivated than I had in years and found a song and music video on YouTube that would fuel my determination—*Hold Me Back*, by Rick Ross. I began devising a plan to get myself out of this particular ditch and never return. I jotted down ideas in a notebook and began making phone calls to executives I'd met along the way. I reconnected with people in powerful positions and fired my attorney and manager to make room for new representation. I needed to be surrounded by people who were excited about me and could see my vision, whatever that vision would be. By my third day in the hotel, I was feeling energized and determined. I was fully focused and looking forward. I knew getting back on my feet would be one of the hardest things I'd ever done in my life, but it wasn't unfamiliar to me. I'd been there before, many times, and I always persevered.

This time, however, would be the last.

I would make the uphill climb back to the top and I would never fall again. I promised myself. I fortified my mind and my heart with prayer and leaned heavily on Deneen for daily spiritual guidance and teaching. There was no way I'd make it out of this time and place in my life and into my truest purpose without clarity, humility, patience, and prayer. I had a lot of making up to do and I was up for the challenge.

Then, I met a man.

Isn't that always how it goes?

Two weeks before I left my apartment and settled into the hotel, I'd been invited to have dinner with a friend at Boa Steakhouse. In passing, I was introduced to Taj. My friend stopped him to say hello as Taj was rushing toward the door, and introduced us. Taj shook my hand, excused himself, and dashed out of the restaurant, leaving his date at the table for over two hours. I didn't know anything about this man, but after watching his date sit alone for so long, I gathered that he must have been a jerk. I never thought about the encounter or him after that. Why would I? We'd barely said two words to each other. But two weeks later, as I sat in my extended-stay hotel room combing through Twitter, following people who had recently followed me, I received a private message from Taj, reminding me we'd met two weeks prior.

I was hesitant to engage.

We sent private messages back and forth for the next four days as he insisted I meet him for lunch or drinks. Eventually, we exchanged phone numbers and began texting one another, before finally talking on the phone. Taj was easy to talk to and he was funny. More than that, he was smart and our conversations soon took an artistic and intellectual turn. He intrigued me and was intrigued by me, but there was so much going on in my life that I didn't have time for another man or for much of anything other than erecting myself. Still, I enjoyed his levity during what was an especially trying period of life.

After nearly running out of money and time at the hotel, Naiim and I packed our bags and headed to a friend's place, deciding to save my last few hundred dollars for food and water. So, we left Woodland Hills and met my friend Tasha at her apartment on the seedier side of Los Angeles. I was instantly nervous as Naiim and I drove through the dilapidated neighborhood. The places and people we passed looked vastly different from what we were accustomed to. Naiim looked shocked by the conditions.

"Don't worry, babe. We won't be here long," I assured him, but I could see the worry in his eyes. "I know it's not what we're used to but we have nowhere else to go right now. I'll think of something. I promise."

CHAPTER TWENTY-ONE

Passion Fruit

efusing to lean on Bruce for financial assistance, I figured I would try to make it on my own for the next two
weeks until my residual checks arrived. It was around
this time I realized there were very few people in my life I could
consider friends. I had a phonebook filled with hundreds of names
and phone numbers of people I barely knew and there were only a
couple people I could call to ask for a place to stay.

So, I swallowed my pride and did just that.

Meanwhile, as I settled into Tasha's apartment, Taj continued
to call and text, asking to meet with me. It was mid-September 2012
and I was staying in the extra room of Tasha's cluttered, unkempt
apartment in a dilapidated part of town, a rough neighborhood in
which I wouldn't usually find myself. But I was there, led to that
place by a chain of events that began over seven years before, and I
couldn't have felt lower.

Naiim and I settled in that first night, but by the next morning I
wanted to get him out of there. I didn't want him to be in that part
of town or in that apartment one moment more than necessary. So,
I drove him to our old neighborhood in the suburbs and dropped

him off at his best friend's house for a few days. I wanted him to have a slice of normalcy in the middle of all the chaos. I felt guilty for having done this to him, to us, and I wanted to do whatever I could to ease his anxieties or fears. Though he never expressed them to me, though he always seemed to trust me and be okay as long as I appeared okay, I knew he felt what I felt. He was my son, and for the past fourteen years we went through everything together.

With Naiim safe, comfortable, and happy at his friend's house in the suburbs, I stopped by the nail salon to have my nails painted. I didn't have much money but with a string of meetings set over the next week, I wanted to look and feel as best as I could. I didn't want people to look at me and be able to tell something was very wrong. All that day, Taj and I spoke on the phone and sent text messages back and forth and, though I had taken a vow to stay focused on the work that needed to be done, I welcomed Taj's distraction from my circumstances. He was sweet and kind when he spoke. I found myself genuinely laughing for the first time in a while. I felt a rush every time my phone chimed with a new message from him or rang when he called. As I was finishing up at the nail salon, we finally made plans to meet for lunch. Suddenly, I had something to look forward to.

I liked that feeling.

Taj allowed me to pick the restaurant and I knew just where to take him. There was this little all-you-can-eat Korean barbecue place tucked away in a small, nondescript shopping mall that I simply adored. It was unassuming and cheap but the food was good. It was a hole in the wall, in stark contrast to the steakhouse where Taj and I first met. I didn't want anything fancy. I arrived first and waited nervously for him to arrive. I wasn't really prepared for a first date. I wore baggy, deconstructed jeans with an oversized T. My hair wasn't done and, as usual, I wore no makeup. When I left Tasha's place, I'd only expected to drop off Naiim, have my nails painted, and then head back to the apartment to figure out my next moves. But Taj insisted we meet that afternoon and I could no longer resist.

Once seated, we ordered raw, thinly sliced meats and vegetables to be cooked over the built-in grill at our table, as well as beers and sake. It was a fun first date as we told stories and asked questions. We knew a lot of the same people and found similarities in our experiences. He was just so funny and my stomach hurt from the belly laughs. We took our time at the restaurant though we were sweating from the incredible heat coming from the burning grills throughout. This particular hole in the wall did not come equipped with air-conditioning, and with the outdoor temperature soaring well into the eighties, the restaurant seemed to have peaked to about 100 degrees.

And all we could do was laugh.

By the end of our lunch, I was smitten. I didn't want to leave Taj and Taj didn't want to leave me. So, we stayed together that day. I parked my car on a side street, hopped into his, and tagged along as he went to the barbershop for a haircut. Then, he took me for frozen yogurt. After that, we settled at the Mondrian hotel for drinks. By then, the sun was soon to set and as we sat near the pool, enjoying the evening breeze, we talked further and more deeply. It was here that I got my first real look at Taj.

He was so handsome to me, though not traditionally so. He had this glimmer of hope in his eyes when he talked about art and creation. We connected as we spoke about the power of writing and the importance of words, of visuals, moving and still pictures, and the conveying of emotion through them. It was here that I discovered I knew his work, the art he made, and in fact knew it quite well. I'd been tracing his fingerprints for a while now, and through his art, I already loved him. He was the director of Rick Ross's *Hold Me Back*, the same music video I'd been using to get me through this terrible time.

Taj had a passion, a fire that had gone out in me years ago. The way he talked about how his work made him feel made me want to feel that way again. I connected with him on a creative level, not because I was able to feel the way he felt but because I remembered what that feeling was like. He was a sculptor, a painter, a man who could take a rib from himself, place it in the dirt, breathe into it, and bring me back to life. I was just that inspired by him.

Feeling comfortable, I confided in Taj as the sun set over West Hollywood. "I'm in between places," I said. "I have a couple weeks until I'm able to find a new place and I'm staying at my girlfriend's apartment in the ghetto somewhere. I hate it there."

"Well, why don't you come stay with me?" Taj suggested, to my delight.

"Really?"

"Yeah! I mean, I'm in the middle of moving, so a lot of my stuff is in storage already, but you're more than welcome to stay for a few days, if that'll help you out."

"It would. It really would."

"Okay, so, you go get your stuff and I'll head over to Target. I need to pick up some sheets, blankets, and towels for you."

"Oh my God. Thank you so much!" I exclaimed as I hugged him tightly. Taj was right on time.

I raced back to Tasha's place and grabbed my bags, which I'd never unpacked. I quickly piled everything into my car and sped over to the Target where Taj was still shopping. I didn't want to lose track of him. By the time he was finished buying supplies, I was pulling up to the store and met with him just in time to follow him home.

He lived in a beautiful high-rise building downtown, overlooking the city. There was very little in the apartment, as he had warned, but there was enough to make me comfortable. "Sit on the couch and don't get up," he ordered as he scampered around the apartment cleaning things and making the bed. He was adorable. Once he was finished, I took a long, hot shower and released all my worries and fears for a while. I slipped into a large T and a pair of black panties, then under the covers as Taj worked in the other room. All the doors in his apartment were made of glass so that, as I lay in bed, I could see him at his desk across the way. I fell asleep watching him and when I awoke around four in the morning, I opened my eyes to see him still at his desk, lit only by the glow of his computer.

He inspired me.

I crept out of bed and tiptoed across the concrete floors and into his office. He looked up at me and smiled, saying nothing. Instinctually, I stood behind him, wrapping my arms around his neck and chest, bending to his neck, kissing it. My hair fell all around him as he let out a sigh, tilted his head, and closed his eyes.

"Come to bed," I whispered.

"In a minute."

For the next three days, Taj and I talked and laughed. He shared his work with me and I shared my ideas with him. He slept very little and seemed to always be working—because he was. Even when he lay in bed, I could feel him still working; his dreams were vivid and his body twitched in his sleep as he held on to me, our bodies never apart.

On the fourth day, I left to pick up Naiim and bring him back with me to meet Taj. The two of them found a certain connection, a camaraderie, as their demeanors were quite similar. It was as if they were the same person, just decades apart. I loved seeing my son smile and laugh with Taj as they got to know each other. Having the three of us there together completed my vision of Taj. I saw him romantically and I saw his potential as a father. I saw him as a friend and a confidant, a peer and a matcher of wits. And as I watched him work in his office into the night and the early hours of the morning, I saw him as a man with vision.

He inspired me every time I awoke from my sleep and found his side of the bed empty. I remembered a small piece of myself whenever he came in from working on a project all night or drew up plans for a new project by the glow of his computer screen between dusk and dawn. I remembered when I'd had that drive, when I'd worked that hard. I remembered what it was like to be commissioned to start and finish a project by a deadline and to pour my heart and soul into it, hardly sleeping until it was done. For all I'd accomplished before meeting Taj, I wanted to be like Taj and to have what he had.

Passion.

Of all the things Aeron took from me, of all the things I gave away, my passion for writing was the most greatly missed. It was the basis of my success and self-sufficiency. Writing was how I coped with life; sharing that life with the world was my way of giving my sorrows, my injustices, and my grievances back to the universe. But now, I couldn't write. I would stare at the blank document on my computer, my cursor blinking, begging for the words. I hadn't written a decent page of anything since I finished *The Vixen Manual* in 2008, before its release in 2009. Even if I'd still had a publishing contract after that, I wouldn't have known what to write; I didn't know what to say. More than not knowing what people wanted from me, I didn't know what *I* wanted from me. All I knew was that I was in this horrible place in my life and I'd been living between hell and purgatory for the past five years. I knew that if I could write, I could write my way out of this place. But each time I poised my fingers on my keyboard, they stalled. Each time I searched for inspiration, it escaped me. Life was too dark, too sad, and nothing and no one moved me.

Until Taj.

Naiim and I left Taj's place five days after I arrived. It was time for Taj to move out, and while a part of me didn't understand why I couldn't go with him, a part of me knew just why. Our five-day first date was over. I cried when I left Taj and I thought about him every day. I longed for him. I longed for the energy he gave me, the spark that ignited between us, the twinkle in his eye when I marveled at his work and the fire in mine. My body missed his at night and my resurgent need for a creative outlet called out for his brilliance. Still, I was charged by the time we spent together and even more determined to get my life back, to find my words and my direction and to write something—anything.

So, I continued making phone calls and taking meetings. I hired a new manager and a new attorney and began thinking of ways to get back to work. But what would I write? What would be the catalyst that would end my writer's block and jump-start my passion? What could possibly undo the emotional damage and blockages caused by the abuse I'd survived over the past five years, the horrible decisions I made, and the hell I'd been through?

The answers were approaching.

CHAPTER TWENTY-TWO

Proof of Life

On September 19, 2012, I received a private message on Facebook from Jillian Bowe, senior editor at Daytime Confidential, asking how Aeron was coping with being let go from his CBS soap opera several weeks prior.

It all began to make sense.

When Aeron came back around, he didn't know I was having trouble keeping my head above water. But he did know that he wouldn't be continuing his stint on the soap opera and he was looking for me to save him. But I couldn't, not again, not anymore, and he could never save me. So, he was content to lie around the apartment, using it as a post in his quest for convenience for as long as he could, before we all had to jump ship. Meanwhile, Bruce sat back and waited for the destruction, for me to learn some sort of lesson.

I did.

After leaving Taj, with nowhere to go and hardly any money left, Naiim and I parked in a familiar neighborhood as the sun began to set, and began falling asleep in the car. In between dozing, I scrolled through my phone, looking for the name of someone I could call for help—someone who wouldn't judge me. I decided on my ex-boyfriend Terry, whom I'd dated and lived with in Phoenix back in 1998 and 1999, before I picked up and moved to Los Angeles without a word. Terry moved to LA just two years later and we kept in touch sporadically over the past eleven years. He was always very supportive of me and had always been there during my roughest times. We hadn't spoken in a couple years but I knew he wouldn't turn me away.

And he didn't.

There was just over a week before I could expect my residual checks in the mail, and Terry said he'd let us crash on the sofa bed in his one-bedroom apartment while I waited. He worked long hours, from evening into the early mornings. He slept a good portion of the day and had weekends off. Naiim and I wouldn't really be in his way and I took to the cooking and cleaning to show my gratitude. Terry had a girlfriend and even though he and I dated way back in the late nineties, we'd never looked at each other in that way again. I was safe with Terry. I'd known him for so long and we had gone through so much together that there was a real history there. He'd known me before I was anybody and he'd known Naiim since he was just one year old. Terry was always a genuine friend and I was relieved to be able to stay with him for the coming week.

But, about four days later, after spending the weekend with his girlfriend, Terry sent me a text message that read, *You and Naiim have to be out by tomorrow. I have a friend coming to stay with me.* My mouth flew open and my heart dropped. I knew what happened; it didn't take a rocket scientist to figure it out. Terry must have told his girlfriend I was staying with him and, intimidated, she demanded I leave.

I replied back, *Okay*. There was nothing I could say or do. I was at the mercy of others and I was the one who put me there.

You guys can stay today and part of tomorrow but I'm going to need you to be gone by the time I get home from work, Terry continued.

Okay, I responded. And with that, Naiim and I packed up and left immediately. I didn't see the point in prolonging the experience nor did I see the point of ever speaking to Terry again. Our long-standing friendship was instantly over and I hoped that, for him, it was worth it. I had just enough money for a day at the hotel and so that's where we were headed. I was still doing my best to not ask Bruce for help, knowing he would only use the opportunity to take advantage of me. So, Naiim and I checked back into the extended-stay hotel and I began making phone calls.

I called Deneen and asked her to pay for one day at the hotel. I called one of my younger sisters and asked the same. They both called the hotel and gave their credit card numbers, making it possible for me to stay there until the checks arrived. I called the UPS Store where my mailbox was housed, every day for several days, asking if my checks were there. For three days, the answer was no. But on October 4, 2012, the answer was yes, and I couldn't drive into the city fast enough!

We were saved!

Armed with around $11,000, I was ready to start my life over and fast, but I soon found out it wouldn't be that easy. There were backed-up bills that needed to be paid and dings on my credit that needed to be rectified before I could move into another apartment. I applied at several places but was denied over and over again. My living situation remained uncertain, so I paid for an extra month of living at the hotel while trying to find a new place and get a handle on the debt that trailed me since my relationship with Aeron. Even though I was finished with him, I still couldn't escape him!

During the first few weeks of October, I continued to fight for my life and livelihood while living in a tiny hotel room with my son. I also continued to see Taj, who moved out of his place and in with a friend, just minutes from the hotel. I tried to write, I did, but nothing happened—maybe a line or two, maybe a paragraph and a half, but nothing more. Everything I wrote was trash and devoid of feeling or meaning. My new representation helped me formulate a book proposal about something I barely cared about and sent it off to publishers. It was only met with more denial. Everywhere I looked, I was being turned down. I was working as hard as I could to make things better. I took comfort that, as hard as things were, at least I didn't have to rely on Bruce for the time being. Still, I was running out of money, and with my rental applications continuing to be denied, I wondered when I would be saved. I wondered how much worse things would get.

It didn't take long to find out.

On the morning of October 26, I awoke with a start. I'd turned off my phone's ringer before going to bed early the night before, but I jumped out of bed that morning feeling frantic, as if there was something wrong. I scrambled around the room, looking for the phone, feeling a sense of urgency. I couldn't remember where I put it. I searched high and low, under the pillows, in the bathroom, on the dresser, only to find it under the bed. Turning on the phone, I saw I missed fourteen calls and twice as many text messages. The missed calls were from friends of mine as well as members of Wayne's crew. My hands began to shake as it became evident something was terribly wrong. I checked the first text message of the bunch. It read, *Wayne is in the hospital.* I'm sure the message contained other words but I wasn't about to waste time reading them.

I called Wayne.

No answer.

I called one member of his crew, then another.

No answer.

No answer.

I called my friend Chris while flinging open my laptop to try to find out what was happening. I was scared. I was shaking and tears weren't far behind.

Chris answered, "Yo."

"What happened?" I asked while searching the Internet.

"Wayne had a seizure or something on the plane . . ."

As he talked, I started reading the news online and I couldn't hear him anymore. I disconnected the call without saying good-bye and started texting Wayne. *Baby, I'm scared. Please let me know you're alright.* I sent the text and waited.

And waited.

Fuck!

Fuck!

Fuck!

I paced around my room, drinking beers for breakfast, worried about my love. I thought about the fights we had in the past and how silly they all seemed in that moment, when I didn't know how sick Wayne was or if he was even alive. I thought about it all. The times I spent with him, the times I spent without him. The joy he brought me. The pain. All that fucking pain! I thought about what I would do without him. What if the next time I lost him, it was forever? I thought about his mortality and mine, and how short life can be. I thought about love and its true definitions, its emotion, its actions— the crazy shit it made us do and say. I paced and I thought. I cried. I drank more. I waited for Wayne to tell me he was okay.

I waited.

And waited.

I'm okay, mama. Sorry I scared you. I love you, the text read when it came in two hours later.

I exhaled for the first time that morning. *Don't be sorry, baby. As long as you're okay, I'm okay. I love you, too.*

Wayne and I texted each other back and forth for the better part of an hour that day and every single day after. He experienced another seizure just days later and I relived my fears all over again, scrambling to get word from inside his camp, waiting for him to tell me he was okay. We never let a day go by after the episodes without saying *I love you*. Not a day went by when I didn't check in on him and he didn't check in on me.

His seizures and the fears and realizations they caused brought us closer. Wayne was always the picture of strength to me. He was *my* strength. He was part of the reason I was happy and healthy again. He was the reason I'd been able to walk away from Aeron and had no intention of settling for Nigel or anyone else beneath my worth. He was the reason I began to eat again, to fill out my jeans and love my body. He made me feel beautiful. He reminded me of who I was and who I was always meant to be. A part of me lived in him, and without him, that part dies.

It was Wayne and his seizures that cracked the ice atop the frozen pool of pent-up anguish and emotion I'd been storing for the past five years. I began to fear and worry about what my life would be like without him. God forbid if something horrible were to happen to him or to me; who would know the truth about us and the love we shared and the heated battles, the falling apart and the coming together? As a writer, as a woman who built her entire life on the telling of truths and the leaving behind of proof of my life, I feared either one of us leaving this earth never having left behind a footprint of our love.

Something was stirring inside me.

I wanted to write it all down.

Still, I could not.

Not yet.

CHAPTER TWENTY-THREE

Wayne's health continued to be touch and go for the rest of October, into November, and beyond. I grew closer to him in that time and my love for him continued to grow—as did my love for Taj. I was disturbed by the feelings I had for Taj and how they seemed to be competing with my feelings for Wayne. It was Taj's mind. It was the conversations we had late at night and the time we spent together that fall. We were incredible. There was a cerebral bond being built and strengthened with each encounter and I found his intelligence incredibly sexy and alluring. Plus, Taj continued to inspire me as I watched him work on project after project, writing, sketching, and designing things, creating images and product for clients around the clock. As an artist, there was very little he couldn't do, and he made me want to create.

Yet, my block remained.

I was still being weighed down by my inability to find a place to live and by my debt. I was running out of time and money, once again, and was continuing to keep my circumstances a secret from most everyone I knew. Taj knew I was living at the hotel but I insisted I was only there while waiting for my apartment to become available and assured him Naiim and I would be moving into our new place before Thanksgiving. It wasn't really a lie. Taj was living with a friend and colleague at the time, not having his own place either, and I think he understood being displaced.

Taj described our relationship as the coming together of lines in a square, bursting with emotion at each sharp point. We were feverish with each other; we were passionate when in each other's arms, when talking about art, theories, and concepts. We were equally as passionate when we argued, and in the span of our short relationship, we found ourselves in quite a few arguments. They were always explosive. But none of our riffs was as explosive as the one we had in early November. As intense as it was, however, I can't remember what the argument was about, as is the case most times we find ourselves arguing with people we love about things that don't matter. Both Taj and I were temperamental and often pushed one another's buttons as we each struggled to find a place for the other in our already complicated lives. Our rage flared as we argued. I sat on the edge of the bed in my hotel room, screaming at him over the phone and listening to him scream at me. And then he said the worst thing anyone has ever said to me, and at the worst time.

"You're such a fucking loser, you know that? You are a loser. You think you are so special and so important; why? Because you wrote a book? You're nothing but a joke and fucking loser!" Taj screamed on the other end of the phone, my mouth agape.

And as I listened to him continue to berate me, I could feel my light being blown out. Whatever I had left, whatever gumption or hope or spirit I had left after all I'd been through, was stolen from me in that moment, and there was nothing I could say. There was no comeback, there was no rebuttal, there was no more fight.

Wounded and dying, I very softly said, "Okay, Taj. I think it's time we get off the phone," and hung up. The tears streamed from my eyes, as I made no sound. They flowed effortlessly and dripped onto my shirt as I turned my phone off and tucked it between the mattress and the box spring. I walked slowly to the light switch on the wall next to the hotel room's door, and flipped it off, then turned out the light on the desk right next to the bed. Sobbing, I crawled under the covers and just lay there.

I couldn't speak. I could barely breathe. There was no one I wanted to talk to and nowhere I wanted to go. I just wanted to be still, so I lay there for the rest of that day and for ten more days after that. Taj had deeply wounded me at a time when I already felt like a loser. I couldn't find my passion to write or a publisher who believed in me. I couldn't find a place to live. I was living hand-to-mouth and had been depending on a man, Bruce, who I believed would only help me in exchange for sexual favors. I was homeless and my son was silently suffering from my instability. I was doing everything I could to stay afloat, living in survival mode, leaning on my instincts, and praying to God, trusting Him and trying not to panic. I was already down and this is when Taj kicked me, in the very rib he gave me. Any inspiration I garnered from him left me like my last breath.

I lay there catatonic for ten days, getting up to prepare food and maybe run to the store for supplies but never with a light heart or a smile on my face. Every move I made was labored and the only thing that felt right was lying down and being very, very still. Every day, I cried and tried to hide my sorrows by doing so in the bathroom of our tiny hotel room. I relied on pillows to stifle the sound of my wails as Naiim spent most of his time on his laptop with his head-phones on, watching movies or playing games online.

And I prayed.

A lot.

I was learning so much about myself during this ordeal. I was learning to talk to God more and to trust Him without fear or doubt. I was learning about the decline of the respect I once had for myself and the respect others had for me, especially the men in my life. I was learning about my resilience and weaknesses. I stayed inside my head for those ten days, thinking about how I got there, to that hotel and to that place in my life. I thought about the choices I made and I thought back to that day in July 2007 when I decided to ignore everything I heard about Aeron and the red flags I saw for myself. I thought about the many chances I had to get out of my relationship with him and how I forced him into my life even though God was so plainly showing me he was not the one. I thought about my obsession with normalcy, family, and how it all must seem to the people on the outside looking in.

I reviewed everything.

It was as if my life was flashing before my eyes as I lay there, catatonic, a shell of who I used to be, getting closer to who I would become. I saw scenes from my life over the past five years and each of them had one common denominator—me. I was at the center of all of it, allowing certain people into my life, ignoring some things and making up other things in my head. I created my own private hell and then perished in the flames.

And on the tenth day, I got out of bed and was reborn.

I jumped up that morning and showered for the first time in days. I opened the window, turned on the lights, played a bit of music, and made breakfast. I was filled with energy and hope and, most importantly, passion. Naiim and I got into the car and headed out to his weekly music class and band rehearsals. Even during the chaos, I tried my best to retain some sort of normalcy and routine for him. I drove down the main drag with music blaring, singing along. Then, I saw something familiar—a shape on the side of the road, a person standing next to his car, talking on the phone. Naiim saw him, too, and smiled. Just as we passed by, his eyes caught ours.

It was Taj.

We hadn't spoken or texted since our fight, and I would have figured that the next time I saw him I'd be overwrought with disgust and anger, but I wasn't. The sight of him made my eyes light up and coaxed a smile bigger than my face could carry. I loved him. I loved him no matter what he said or did and it surprised me. Quickly, I reached for my phone and called him.

"Hey, I just saw you guys!" he said as he answered the phone.

"Yeah. You saw us?" I asked, still grinning.

"I saw Naiim first, and his big smile, then I saw you. Where are you guys going?"

"I'm taking Naiim to class and rehearsals."

"Okay, well, hit me when you get back to this side of town."

"I will. It was good to see you."

"Good to see you, too."

There was just something about Taj and my relationship with him, something that had begun the very first day we spent together. I already loved him more than I could ever be mad at him, and no matter how much he hurt me, that love wouldn't change. Until I met Taj, the only man I loved this unconditionally was Wayne. It frightened me to love someone else so completely, as well as warmed my heart to know I could.

After all I'd been through, I wasn't broken.

It was no coincidence that I met Taj that night at the steakhouse or that he found and contacted me just days after I settled in the hotel. It wasn't happenstance that he moved out of his place and wound up in the same suburban neighborhood Naiim and I wound up in, at the exact same time, about forty-five minutes from where either of us had been living before. And now, it wasn't a coincidence that he happened to be standing outside a restaurant, talking on his phone, waiting for his food, just when I passed by after ten days of solitude. Taj and I were being drawn toward one another and there was nothing we could do about it.

That morning, I woke up feeling good, but after talking to him, I felt even better. There was no animosity between us and that just fueled my newly rediscovered passion further. Wayne's illness had stirred my emotions, Taj's creativity had ignited mine, and Taj's harsh words had temporarily broken my spirit, but in those ten days since, I had become stronger in the broken places. Taj built me up just to break me down, and the straw that broke my back and sent me into a catatonic state soon served as kindling.

My passion would finally catch fire.

CHAPTER TWENTY-FOUR

Mercy

By the next morning, I knew just what to do. I went to the grocery store for a six-pack of Japanese beer, came back to the room, and sat at the desk. I opened my laptop and a bottle of beer, plugged in my headphones, pressed play on a play-list filled with Wayne's songs, and began to write. *How to Make Love to a Martian* was born in that cramped hotel room, in the middle of a series of crises, at a time when I had no idea what the future held for me. With all that was swirling around—the rejection, the wandering, the instability of my life and relationships—I honed in on the one person I feared losing the most.

Wayne.

The idea of someone you love being sick and the possibility of them dying, today or any day, somehow manages to override any fear, worry, or doubt you may feel for yourself. My heart was filled, not with sorrow for my own circumstances, but with love and appreciation for Wayne, now more than ever, and I had to write it down. I had to leave it behind for someone to read, so others would know that Wayne and I were here and that we loved. Ironically, it was the hateful words of my other lover that broke my writer's block and sent me on this journey to recap my five-and-a-half-year relationship with Wayne.

The words poured out as the music played. I couldn't stop my fingers from hitting the keys at eighty words a minute. I entered a zone, a parallel place in my mind; I stared at the screen, barely ever looking down at the keyboard. I was writing for the first time in four years and I didn't want it to stop! I was obsessed with the book for three days, almost forgetting the world around me until I received a call from David, the manager of an apartment property about which I'd inquired online. It was the only thing that could make me stop writing.

I made an appointment to see an available unit in David's building the following day. It was about two weeks before Thanksgiving and I promised my son we would have a place to live before the holidays. I prayed to God and begged Him to help us find a home by then and I never doubted it would happen, being careful not to override my faith with fear, just as Deneen taught me. I wanted God to know I trusted Him and no longer wanted to fight against His will. From that point on, I only wanted what was best for me.

So, I kept my spirits high and my faith higher.

The small courtyard-style apartment building was perfect. As David and I entered the breezeway on our way to the unit, I was overwhelmed by a feeling of peace and tranquility. Lush gardens and bubbling fountains calmed me instantly. The suburban location of the building was just what we needed and the price of the unit was spot on. There was nothing about the building or the unit that didn't fit my hopes or expectations. So, despite my poor credit and recent eviction, I confidently filled out an application. David ran my credit and checked my references. I kept a good relationship with one of the managers of my prior apartment complex; though I'd broken my lease, she didn't know why, as I'd cited my reason for leaving as the recent flea and roach infestation in my unit that had gone unchecked. So, she gave me a good reference. My credit wasn't the best, but David overlooked that and focused instead on the six-figure income I made the year before and claimed on my taxes. I

waited on pins and needles for days, working to get David everything he needed to fulfill my application. Then, just one week before
Thanksgiving, my application was approved!

But there was just one problem—I was already nearly out of
money, again. I gave David the $500 deposit and I still had to write a
check for $1,900 more by my move-in date. Then there was the cost
of the movers, the closing bill for my storage unit, and the money I
had to pay to turn on the utilities. I needed help. So, begrudgingly,
and out of other options, I called Bruce.

"I think I'm going to get a hotel room at the Intercontinental.
Wanna meet me there?" Bruce proposed. He never came right out and
said what he was doing. He always beat around the bush and acted
as if what was going on between us was something other than what
it was. I really just wanted him to say, "Oh. You need money? Cool.
Come fuck me and I'll give it to you." But the nature of our relationship wasn't something I think he wanted to admit or even say out loud.
Some people are too ashamed to admit what they do, but not enough
to stop doing it. This time, however, I had a trick up my sleeve.

Naturally, I wouldn't leave Naiim alone in the hotel to go pick
up the money from Bruce at another hotel way across town. What
loving mother would? So, he and I piled into the car and made the
trek across town in rush-hour traffic. It took us nearly two hours to
get there. On the way, Bruce continuously called to check on my
progress and I alerted him I was inching ever closer, never mentioning I was with Naiim.

I pulled into the hotel's drive, and as the valet opened my car
door, I assured him, "You can leave it here. I'm just picking up a
package and I won't be long." Naiim and I made our way through
the hotel's lobby, into the elevator, and to Bruce's room. I knocked
lightly, and as Bruce answered the door, his eyes opened wide to find
me standing there with my son. I smirked.

"I can't stay long," I said as we entered the room. "Valet is holding my car and Naiim needs to get to bed." Naiim stayed close to
the door, his intuition telling him Bruce was up to no good with his
mother.

"Come in, Naiim. Have a seat!" Bruce said.

"I'm good," Naiim insisted.

"Yeah, I wasn't about to leave him in the hotel by himself. It's a derelict hotel with all sorts of questionable people coming in and out of there. It wouldn't be right," I explained, still smirking. I had him between a rock and hard place. If he refused to give me the money now, he would essentially be admitting that our relationship was based solely on sex and that if he couldn't have sex with me, he wouldn't help me—in front of my son. And he couldn't very well demand I have sex with him when my son was in the other room.

Naiim and I only stayed for a few minutes as Bruce peeled $2,000 from a large stack of hundred-dollar bills and handed it to me. I knew this wouldn't be the last time I had to deal with Bruce, but at least for the moment, he wouldn't be allowed to take advantage of me. Back in the elevator, as Naiim and I headed back down to valet, I smiled. I hadn't won the war, but this small victory was mine.

I didn't have to break my promise to Naiim.

He and I moved into our new apartment the day before Thanksgiving.

It seemed as if my luck was beginning to take a turn for the better. Still, I was far from fully recovered from the damage done over the past five and a half years. Now that Naiim and I were in our new place, I had to fight hard to keep it, and since I was still receiving rejections from the nearly thirty publishers to which I submitted book proposals, I would still need Bruce to help me survive. Even though my writer's block had lifted and I was in the middle of writing *How to Make Love to a Martian*, it wasn't a book I wanted to sell to a publisher to have printed and promoted around the world. *Martian* was a very intimate, personal project, and though I wanted to share it with my fans and Wayne's, I didn't want to profit greatly from it, especially at a time when his health was so delicate.

Instead, I was submitting something less personal.

Not *every* publisher turned me down outright. There were a few who may not have wanted to publish the safe and practical relationship guide I submitted but who were sure to respond with requests for what they really wanted from me. As one publisher asked, "Can she submit a list of men?"

A list of men.

There I was, having fought for my life for over five years—having been dragged through the mud by an abusive husband, having fallen apart at the seams, starved myself, and struggled to break free—and when it finally seemed there may be a way out from under the rubble of what used to be my life, I was being asked for a list of men!

What kind of list did they want? A list of the cabdrivers I'd met during my travels? Or maybe they wanted a list of all the waiters and maître d's that had filled my empty wine glasses over the years. My gardener, pool man, gynecologist? What exactly were they asking me?

My agent tried his best to make the request seem less insulting than it was, but it was clear—the gossip and rumors that had been swirling around about me for the past handful of years were affecting my ability to get work. I wanted to write about something real, something true to my life and important to me. I was no longer a twentysomething with a long history to tell. I was well into my thirties, a divorcée and single mother, a woman who had lost everything she worked so hard to achieve, a domestic abuse survivor, and now a starving author, dying to work.

I could have sold out and given in to what those publishers wanted from me but I figured I'd done that before. From the very beginning, I'd given my publishers and even a sector of my readers what *they* wanted, going against everything I wanted for my life and career. *Confessions* wasn't meant to be my first book; I was pitching *The Vixen Manual*. I didn't want to write *The Vixen Diaries*; I was still rooting for *The Vixen Manual*! And with *Diaries*, I felt forced to reveal the name of the character in *Confessions* known as Papa, after my editor threatened I'd have to return the $250,000 advance if I didn't. Then there was *SatisFaction*, the book I had nothing to do with. I hated the topic, the title and subtitle, and the cover, and I didn't even write it! So much of my career had been built on what other people wanted of me, and at the end of it all, I was the only one who'd lost. Everything had been so contrived and choreographed. There were dozens of people with their hands in my books, making decisions without me, and my writing had become less about me and more about satisfying the machine. I was determined to move forward in my career and to rebuild my life, but do so with integrity and by writing only about the things that were important me, staying true to my art and to myself.

So, I turned down those publishers who wanted this phantom list of men they thought I'd been collecting over the years. As I grew older, I grew wiser, and my relationships became more substantial. Though I wasn't living the sort of wild, sex-crazed life the public imagined, I did have very important people in my life that I wanted to protect. My private life actually became private. Still, there had to be something I was willing to write that would interest a publisher.

All I needed was one.

In the meantime, I continued to depend on Bruce, humbling myself to his possessive, demeaning treatment of me. By December 2012, just three months after my residual checks had come in and three months until the next ones would arrive, I was completely out of money and was back to leaning on Bruce to help me with rent, groceries, and monthly bills. On the third of December, he asked if I needed help and I admitted I did before he agreed to take care of my monthly expenses. Days went by and then weeks. Soon, it was the twenty-sixth of the month and my new landlord was growing increasingly impatient. I called and texted Bruce for three weeks straight but he never responded. This was his usual game—to offer help and then keep me waiting, begging for money.

I was practicing faith and patience and praying but by the end of the month, I'd had enough with the psychological and financial abuse. If Bruce really wanted to help me, he should have done so by then and not had me waiting and begging for weeks. Fed up, I sent him a text message.

I've been calling you for three weeks and I haven't heard from you. You offered to help me and then disappeared! No matter how badly I need the help, I'm not going to continue to beg for it. Either you're going to do it or you're not. But don't have me depending on you all this time if you're not going to come through. I could have been working on another way to get it done instead of trying to track you down for almost a month!

It didn't take long for Bruce to respond. After not hearing from him in all that time, it took exactly one irate text message to get him to answer me. He called my phone right away and as I answered, all I could hear was yelling. We bantered back and forth for several minutes, pleading our cases. Whatever he was saying went in one ear and out the other and his words were quickly forgotten, except for a few.

"How do I know you're not going to do the same shit you did to me at my other apartment? You knew I needed the rent and you knew how much I needed, and you promised to help me but you purposely shorted me! That's how I wound up getting evicted! And now this! Now you want me to fucking beg for the help you offered me? How much of this shit do you expect me to take?" I yelled, tears streaming down my cheeks.

"Well, I wasn't about to pay for some other motherfucker to lay his head in your apartment, and what you need to realize is that sometimes you have to beg for what you want when you're at someone else's mercy!" Bruce responded, sternly.

And there it was.

Finally, Bruce admitted that he shorted me on purpose. In that moment, he proved how much pleasure he got from dismantling my life and from my begging for his help. His words rang in my ears, playing themselves back over and over again. This was it; this was where it had all led me. Silently, I vowed to never forget those words and to hold them against Bruce, always. But that was not the moment to buck against him; I needed his money too much. So, I grit my teeth, bore the abuse, and did whatever it took to take care of my son and me.

CHAPTER TWENTY-FIVE

Do the Work

Naiim and I made it through the holidays and the New Year, though there was no real celebration—no Christmas tree, no gifts—and when his fifteenth birthday came around in mid-January, there just wasn't enough money to celebrate. Bruce was only handling the basics and using my body up in the process. He was still with his fiancée, who lived in another state and had a personal life of her own. Everyone who witnessed their relationship knew it was a sham, and I picked up the slack, doing all the things a girlfriend or fiancée would: being there for him all hours of the day and night, listening to him gripe, supporting his career moves, staying up late nights watching television, and joking around. Bruce continued to talk about our relationship as if it were so magical and heartwarming and I wondered if he thought he was buying my affections. I fucking hated him for the way he treated me, and the power he exacted because of his ability to help me through one of the roughest periods of my life. I vowed to work even harder and looked forward to the day I would be free of him, just as I'd gotten free from Aeron.

The winter and spring of 2013 was somewhat uneventful. I continued to struggle a bit in the beginning. I entered into an option continuation deal with Fox Television Studios for *Confessions* and kept myself afloat by self-publishing *How to Make Love to a Martian* in February. Priced at only $2.99, the project wasn't something I was trying to get rich from, and I turned down most interview requests about it. I really just wanted to create something that was completely mine, a book that hadn't been riffled through by editors and influenced by a publishing conglomerate. And I wanted to make a moderate amount of money to hold me until I could find the right book and the right publisher. I wasn't trying to be greedy. I just wanted to be fair. Besides, I was happy just to have broken through my writer's block, knowing that, having done so, I could write anything else I wanted as soon as I knew what that should be.

Over the first half of 2013, I did everything I could to support myself and need Bruce less and less until I didn't need him at all. Between proceeds from *Martian*, my payments from Fox, and my ever-faithful residual checks, I was able to take care of myself more often than not. By the summer, I was feeling like myself again and started hanging out with friends for the first time in years. I spent most of the summer poolside, eating and drinking and dancing. I was healthy and less stressed and I was coming alive again. Gone were the days of eating disorders, loneliness, and sadness. I was enjoying life with fewer financial woes. I was silly and lighthearted and laughing more than I had in years.

That May, my divorce from Nigel became final after more than a year of confusion, missed filings, and incomplete paperwork. He and I managed to stay in contact while working our way through the blunder-filled proceedings. Eventually, he hired an attorney who, after a few blunders of her own, brought us before a judge for the final stamp of approval. The process couldn't have been messier if the Three Stooges had handled it, but it was all done that summer and I was finally free!

Taj and I continued to see each other and grew closer, forming a bond that had become unbreakable. I watched him build a company and a brand with such passion that the feeling was infectious. I became obsessed with building a new brand of my own, only just then realizing that having a slew of products didn't mean I had a brand! I dove into business books and magazines. I paid close attention to the backstories of successful people, brands, and companies, and I thought long and hard about what I wanted for myself. I thought about the mistakes I made in my personal and professional life and found that I could have avoided nearly a decade of heartbreak if, in making any decision, I would have asked myself just one question:

And then what?

I had gone about life never asking myself about the future, never thinking about the consequences before making decisions. If I would have only asked myself *And then what?*, everything could have been different. So, by the fall of 2013, I was determined to make every decision count and not take one step before asking myself, *And then what?*

With Taj as a major motivator, I began building my brand, doing so based on the things that interested me and not necessarily based on what interested a portion of my audience. I wanted to build something that would be easy to maintain because it was organic, true to who I am. I wanted to finally show people what my real interests were and what my actual quality of life was. So, I began developing the Karrine & Co. brand and its subsidiaries, planning a long-term strategy and outlook for each company. I spent plenty of nights burning the midnight oil, much the way I saw Taj do when I was with him. I mimicked his drive and was inspired every time I watched him work, or talked with him about his work, and my drive was often influenced by his. I was working harder than I had in years and it felt good.

Still, there was just one thing missing—one very important thing—the perfect book.

With 2014 just months away, it dawned on me that in less than two years, *Confessions of a Video Vixen* would be ten years old, and I felt as if that book deserved to be commemorated. *Confessions* had changed my life and afforded me everything I ever dreamed of as a child. It had taken me around the world and launched a career and far-reaching recognition. To this day, I still reap its rewards. Once I realized the tenth year was fast approaching, I knew the next book and deal had to be commemorative. I contacted my representatives, told them the plan, and prepared the proposal for the book you're reading right now. Within weeks, the new proposal was sent out to tens of agents and I waited anxiously for their replies, fingers crossed.

Many denied it.

A few wanted that fabled list of men.

But there were biters, and for the first time in over four years there were publishing offers on the table and all I had to do was choose.

And I did.

As I slowly began putting the pieces of my life back together, I never forgot the horrible things Bruce and Taj said to me. I never forgot what it felt like to be called a loser and to be told I had to beg because I was at someone else's mercy. I constantly reminded myself what it felt like to not be in control of my life and instead be at the mercy of men. I kept in mind the decisions I made back in 2007 and how choosing to be with Aeron had cast a dark shadow over my life for all those years. I thought about all I lost and all I gave away, realizing I'd always had the power to change my life but had chosen to relinquish it. I knew I wouldn't be making that choice again.

In October 2013, I was on the precipice of signing my first book deal in four years and looking forward to the year ahead. My relationship with Wayne was the same as it had always been, with its highs and lows, falling outs and coming togethers, but we were stronger than ever. I was still in love with him after everything. My relationship with Taj was blossoming and we were finally to the point where we could admit we loved each other and wanted to be in each other's lives for the long haul. I loved him differently than I loved Wayne but just as unconditionally. My relationship with Bruce changed as I gained more independence. I continued to loathe him but wanted to keep him around long enough for him to witness me get back on my feet without him. But the strongest relationships in my life were those with my son, my God, and myself. Together, we made it through one of the most trying times of my life and we were closer than ever.

It was important that my son see his mother pull it together, gather her resources, and make it happen for us again. I wanted him to know that I'm not perfect, that I make mistakes, but that I can also make them right. I wanted him to know that I would not be making the same mistakes twice—not anymore. We were moving forward and were not going to miss out on life, again. So, that October, I signed a new publishing contract and officially started my life over, one more time.

I was happy.

I was elated!

I was walking on fucking air!

I was having more meaningful relationships, I was stabilizing financially, I was looking and feeling better than I had in years, and I just signed a lucrative deal that was sure to put me back on my feet for the long run. I was able to pay back family and friends who sent me money during my hard times and I was able to continue avoiding Bruce's sexual advances. It was the happiest I'd been since 2007. I was glowing, and apparently giving off a radiance that could be felt for miles because, in mid-December, Aeron came lurking—no doubt having seen a blip of my joy on his seek-and-destroy radar.

CHAPTER TWENTY-SIX

Apropos

*I*t was around December 15, 2013, when I received a cryptic email from my first ex-husband. It read, *I need to talk to you before both of us make a mistake we can't take back*. Instantly, I knew what Aeron was up to; it was the same shit he always did, that radar he had that sent him into attack mode, never wanting me to be happy. For a few days, we played phone tag and then on December 19 made plans to meet for brunch at a restaurant near my apartment, a place we'd frequented often when we were married.

I went into the situation quite snide as I was in the midst of preparing to leave town with Taj in a few days. He and I were in a really great place and this would be our first trip together to spend time with his friends and family. Floating on a cloud, I made my way to the restaurant as slowly as I could and arrived about fifteen minutes late, even though the eatery was just two minutes from my place. Aeron had arrived on time and waited for me.

Before leaving the apartment, I preened; I wanted to be sure to look my very best. I wore a form-fitting outfit and five-inch heels. I did my makeup and perfected my hair. I wanted to stun my

ex-husband; I wanted him to see I was not only okay but thriving—
that I was happy, healthy, and gorgeous without him.

I walked into the restaurant and scanned the room, finding him
as he stood up, his six-foot-four-inch frame towering. I gave a half
smile and made my way over to him, greeting him with a one-handed
hug and a lazy hello. We sat across from each other in a booth and
made the usual pleasant conversation for the first few minutes.

"You look beautiful," Aeron started.

"Thank you. You look like shit. I can tell you haven't been sleeping," I responded with a smirk. "Your skin looks good, though!
You've been in a steam room, huh?"

"Yeah, I was just in a steam room yesterday. And it's hard to
sleep these days."

"Oh, yeah? Why is that?"

"I'm not happy, Karrine."

Just then, the waitress came by. "Hi there, you two ready to
order?"

Completely unmoved by Aeron's admittance of unhappiness, I
ordered a large breakfast and a mimosa. I was starving and something told me I was going to need to be tipsy for this conversation.

Aeron ordered his food and as the waitress walked away, he continued. "You were right. The way you had it all set up before, the
way you took care of the kids, the house, and me was all right. I just
couldn't see it then. I want it all back."

"You want what back?" I asked, already knowing the answer.

"I want *you* back. I want the regimen you had in place. I want to
go to bed early and turn off the phone for family time. I want to go
to church and brunch on Sundays and not run around town taking
meetings that amount to nothing. Just like you always insisted."

"Really? What brought this on?"

"I'm just not happy, babe, and I want my wife back. I need you
to fix my life."

"Fix your life? What's wrong with your life?" I asked as our food
was delivered to the table. "I'll need another mimosa," I said to our
waitress.

"Things are just out of control and they were never like this when we were together."

"Yeah, because I was a good wife who took complete care of you, your son, our home, and everything else. But you didn't appreciate any of it. You didn't want to be there! You didn't want to be told what to do or to be regimented! That's what you said back then, so don't change your fucking song now!" I insisted, a sarcastic tone in my voice.

"I know. I know!"

"You wanted to let your mother run your life instead, so go let your *mother* fix your life."

"I don't really talk to my mother anymore. I know she came in between us in our relationship and ruined a lot of things for me and for us but she's not around as much. She moved into a new place and finally got a life of her own." He was trying to entice me. He thought he was saying what I wanted to hear.

"Mmm. Enough about that. How's Jonah?"

"He's okay. He's in Chicago with his mother."

"Oh, good! He's there for the holidays?"

"Yeah. Well, he's out there for good, at least for right now."

"For good? The judge finally granted her custody?"

"Yeah, but I'm fighting it." After six years of a heated court battle, after all Aeron's lies, antics, and deceptions, Jonah's mother was finally able to regain custody of her son after a Chicago court found him unfit.

I nodded my head but smiled on the inside, thinking about when Aeron tried to have my son taken away from me, knowing his chickens had come home to roost. "Well, good for him. Every child deserves to be with its mother. I mean, she has a house and a husband, and they have four or five other children between them. So, he's with his family and he's stable now!"

"I would have never lost him if I was still with you, though."

"This is true, but you fucked all that up. You had a wife and a stable home, you had two kids and all the love and support in the world. But you wanted to do what you wanted to do. You wanted to be gone days, weeks, and months at a time!"

"I was never gone for months!"

"Aeron," I continued, putting down my fork and looking him square in the eyes, "you were gone for *seven* months one time, and you don't remember half the shit you did or the damage you caused, because you and I were in two different relationships. You got to fuck shit up and just walk away and I was left to try to pick up all the fucking pieces, to repair the broken spirits and emotional gashes you left behind! Then, whenever you got tired or bored or thought for one second I might be moving on, you came back to fuck shit up, again! You had everything and you ruined it. You fucked up your life and you have to be okay with that now. I will never come back to you. You were my biggest mistake and the worst thing that ever happened to me. And I'm sorry to hear you're so unhappy but that's your fault and, as for me, I am happier without you. In fact, I've never been so happy! And I'm sitting here, listening to you, and all you have done for the past hour is tell me all the things I can do for you. You have never once offered to do anything for me! You've just come back around here to take, to bleed me dry, to finish me off. You haven't once asked about me, how I'm doing, because you don't even care!"

My tone was serious but my voice remained low and calm. I was in control. I was confident and secure and, for the past fifteen months, had never once regretted my decision to leave Aeron behind.

"I do care, babe. That's why I wanted to talk to you. I mean, there were lots of good times and all you choose to remember are the bad times! We were happy, we were in love, and I can't imagine starting my life over with someone else. The woman I'm seeing now wants to get married and have kids and I'd rather do those things with you. I figured it was time we gave it another chance."

"I think you should stay with your new girlfriend and marry her and have kids with her. I'm sure she deserves you more than I do," I responded, laughing at his attempt to make me feel as if I'd better jump on his offer before someone else snatched him up. I giggled like a child as I asked, "How long have you been dating this person?"

"About two months."

I fucking roared! My mimosa almost came through my nose, I laughed so hard! "Child, you should marry that girl you've known for two months and go live happily ever after."

"But I'd rather be with you!"

"Yeah, I bet! But I'm not the same girl you used to know. Besides, you haven't even thought to ask me what's going on with me—if I'm in a relationship or not. As usual, you're just assuming I've been sitting around fucking waiting for you to come back into my life!" My laughter was uncontrollable. I couldn't take it anymore. He was being too ridiculous.

Aeron looked at me blankly, searching for his next line, his next lie. He was still the same man, the same abuser trying to fool me into falling into the pit with him again. This time, he'd lost everything. The year before, he'd been cast on a popular sitcom but that character soon played out, and Aeron found himself working less and less. To make matters worse for him, he had lost custody of Jonah. Plus, he looked like shit. He was exactly where he deserved to be—and so was I.

"Well, this has been lovely, but I have to go. I still have some shopping to do before my boyfriend and I leave town in a few days," I said, trying to end the date.

"Oh, you have a boyfriend?"

"Yeah, and you would have known that an hour ago if you would have asked anything about me and my life. We've been together over a year. Anyway, good luck with your relationship. I hope that works out for you."

We rose from our seats and walked out of the restaurant to the parking lot and stood next to my new car, just two spaces away from his dinged and dated vehicle.

"Well, maybe we can continue to talk. We can build and start over slowly. Nothing's wrong with that, right?" Aeron questioned. He was still looking for a way in.

"Sure. Email me," I responded, one foot already in my car.

"Aren't you going to give me a hug good-bye?"

"Ugh. Okay," I whined, as I stepped in front of him and gave him another one-handed hug and two pats on the back.

"Don't fucking pat my back like we were never married!"

"Sweetie, we weren't."

"Oh, yeah?" Aeron said as he leaned in and tried to kiss my lips. I couldn't believe it! He was still trying to lure me into his web with all the same bullshit he gave me in 2007.

I moved my face as he chased my lips from side to side, holding me in an embrace. "Stop! I'm not kissing you!"

"You're my wife! Kiss me!"

I pushed away from Aeron and said, sternly, "I'm not your wife, anymore. You divorced me, remember? And you have to be okay with that, too."

Aeron reached into his pocket and tried one more trick, one more last-ditch effort to win my affections. He pulled out a short stack of money and peeled off a few hundred-dollar bills. "Well, here. Maybe I wasn't always able to help you out as much as you needed me to, but I can do a little something now."

I took the money. "Thanks."

"Buy something for Naiim for Christmas and tell him it's from me."

"Will do!" I said as I closed my car door and started my vehicle.

"Call me later. I love you."

"Bye!" I yelled out the window as I backed up and sped out of the parking lot, leaving Aeron in my dust. Literally.

I shoved the money into my purse and laughed. There was no way I would buy my son a Christmas gift on Aeron's behalf. There was no way I would ever tell my son I even met with Aeron. I wasn't going to infect my kid with so much as a mention of that monster's name, and the fact that Aeron wanted me to was further proof that nothing about him was different. I took the $300 he gave me and went shopping for my trip with Taj.

It seemed apropos.

The Beginning

*I*t's been a wild ten years since the publication of my first memoir, *Confessions of a Video Vixen*, but it probably wasn't the sort of wild ride you imagined. Maybe you thought there would be lots of men and sex, drugs, and random regrets in this book. Maybe you thought there'd be tabloid-worthy romps and gross sexual misjudgments, or baskets of other people's dirty laundry. Maybe you expected the words in this book to be less important.

But I couldn't write about things that didn't happen.

With anyone's life, there is always speculation from outsiders and rumors swirling around, others trying to imagine what they think your life is like. But the outsiders are always wrong. Sometimes we can project a perfect picture of strength and resilience, never leading on that we are broken and closing in on our deaths.

We all have a persona.

People who don't know us, who only see us at work, follow us on social media, or hear of us through conversations with other people who don't know us, gather bits and pieces of information, whether true or false, and use that information to make their minds up about us.

They condemn.

Sometimes that condemnation even comes from those we know and love, who we thought knew and loved us.

All of us want to believe we are different and that is exactly what makes us all the same. Some people believe they are better than others and it is that belief that makes them worse. I am not alone and as I gathered my thoughts to write this book, I struggled with its angle, I struggled with its format, but I did not struggle with its truths. You needed to know this. Those of you who have never been struck, never been choked, never been spit upon and called names you couldn't repeat, you needed to know that this exists and no one is immune. You needed to know what it does to a person. And those of you who *have* been abused, you needed to know that you are not alone, and in a split second, you can change your life by changing your mind. You all needed to know that one bad decision could ruin your life, for years or forever.

You needed to know it happened to me.

You needed to know you, too, can make it through.

The journey to regain my emotional, financial, and physical footing was a tough one. There were a slew of lessons along the way, all of which I have heeded and all of which I remind myself of daily. I no longer desire to make things look good or acceptable to others. I no longer believe I can buy happiness, and I put more stock in the love of God, my son, and those closest to me than in anything else. I live my life peacefully, surrounded by loved ones with good intentions, quickly discarding anyone who tries to abuse my friendship, my love, or me.

I have been made better, stronger, and more aware.

As for the Vixen, she never existed, and what remains after the chewing up and spitting out of my past persona is this—I am a woman, faulty and flawed, but a woman nonetheless. I deserve better than I have accepted in the past and I deserve all that's amazing in my future.

Thank you for spending the past ten years with me.

Thank you for waiting for me to step into my true light and purpose.

Thank you for accompanying me all the way to the beginning.

ABOUT THE AUTHOR

Karrine Steffans is the *New York Times* best-selling author of six titles: *Confessions of a Video Vixen*, *The Vixen Diaries*, *The Vixen Manual*, *SatisFaction*, *How to Make Love to a Martian*, and *Decor and the Single Girl*.

Karrine and her books have been featured on shows hosted by Paula Zahn, Donny Deutsch, Tyra Banks, Bill O'Reilly, Geraldo Rivera, Kathy Lee Gifford, Hoda Kotb, and the queen of daytime herself, Oprah Winfrey. Quite accidentally, the author also contributed a satirical editorial to HBO's *Real Time with Bill Maher*.

Karrine continues to lecture at universities nationwide and volunteers her time serving causes supported by the United Nations, the International Labour Organization, and others with special interest in women's rights, modern-day slavery, and trafficking.

ALSO BY KARRINE STEFFANS AND PUBLISHED BY BENBELLA BOOKS

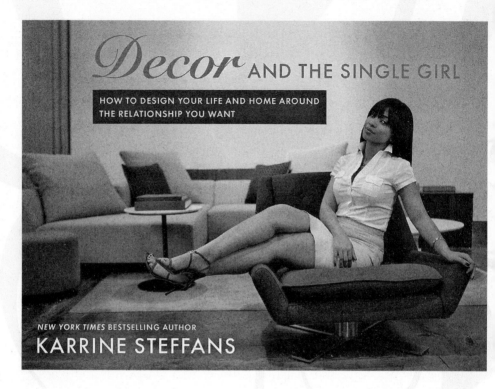

Decor and the Single Girl, by *New York Times* bestselling author Karrine Steffans, is a beautifully photographed guide for today's single woman ready to make room in her life for a man. But, before she makes that room, she has to decorate it—and not for the life she has, but for the life she wants!

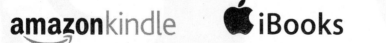